LADIES COUTURE
TAILORING

To Freda
Best wishes
Michelle Pye.

Michelle Pye

LADIES COUTURE
TAILORING

A STEP-BY-STEP
PRACTICAL GUIDE
TO MAKING A JACKET
THAT FITS

THE CROWOOD PRESS

First published in 2021 by
The Crowood Press Ltd
Ramsbury, Marlborough
Wiltshire SN8 2HR

enquiries@crowood.com

www.crowood.com

British Library Cataloguing-in-Publication Data
A catalogue record for this book is available
from the British Library.

ISBN 978 1 78500 916 7

Cover design: Sergey Tsvetkov

Photographs by Michelle Pye and Wendy Pye.

All products used in this book were
purchased from:
English Couture Company
18 The Green
Syston
Leicestershire
LE7 1HQ
www.englishcouture.co.uk

Typeset by Sharon Dainton Design
Printed and bound in India by Parksons Graphics Pvt. Ltd., Mumbai.

Dedication

This book is dedicated to my late parents,
Jack (John) and Iris Pye. Without their
amazing support throughout the years I
would not be where I am today.
Secondly, it is dedicated to my sister
Wendy. Without her unending patience
and organizational and photographic
skills, this book would never have been
finished.

Contents

Introduction   7

01 Equipment and Materials   9

02 Choosing the Pattern and Fitting with the Toile   21

03 Pattern Alterations   31

04 Cutting Out   49

05 Joining the Pieces   61

06 The Pockets   67

07 The Foundations of the Jacket   79

08 The Collar   97

09 The Sleeves   103

10 Hand-Finishing   113

11 Pressing Off and Final Touches   121

Appendix   124

Glossary of Tailoring Terms   125

Index   126

Introduction

'Tailoring is an art but it's also a dying trade.' Those were the words of a local tailor to my mother when she told him that I had a job in a tailor's workroom in my home town of Leicester.

He was partly right, of course; tailoring is an art, and a properly tailored jacket is something quite beautiful. I have a theory about the second part of his statement. Tailors are very secretive people and will not pass on their skills willingly. Only the people working in their workroom will be privileged to any information and even then, only the bits they need to complete their jobs. Tailors also try to make things extremely complicated to the outside world, so people think it's too hard and give up before they get the chance to give it a go.

The way fashion has gone recently doesn't help either. There are fewer and fewer reasons to wear tailored clothes, but I always feel so good when I'm wearing a jacket or coat that I have made. I enjoy every minute spent sewing a jacket or coat, even the boring but vital fitting stages. The satisfaction of saying 'I made it' when someone asks, 'Where did you get that jacket?' is second to none.

The most common question I'm asked is, 'What is the difference between a dressmaker and a tailor?'

- A dressmaker will sew together the pieces of fabric and trust the pattern will create the shape.
- A tailor will cut the pattern pieces from the fabric and mould them to the shape required.

There are many ways to tailor a jacket and if you went into each tailor's shop on Savile Row in London, you would come across many ways of doing the same thing. Each tailor would swear his method is the only way of doing it.

This book contains the methods I learnt in my seven years in a gentlemen's tailoring workroom and the adaptions I have made to that method whilst making for my mainly female customers and teaching students. I have broken down each stage into easy bite-size pieces, so everyone who has dressmaking skills can have a go and make a perfectly wearable jacket.

I know that it will fit you better and be made of a better-quality fabric and that the making-up will be of a higher standard than anything you will buy in the shops.

Another question I'm asked is, 'How long does it take to make a jacket?' Unless you are working in the workrooms with a deadline over you, I usually say, 'I love every minute I spend tailoring so enjoy it, however long it takes.'

I hope this book will inspire you to have a go at making a jacket and that it gives you as much enjoyment as I have every time I make and wear a handmade jacket.

Note 1:
I have given the measurements in this book in both metric and imperial. The conversion of these measurements is not precise. You can use either system of measurement but don't start out using one system and move to the other or your measurements won't be accurate.

Note 2: Instructions are for right-handed readers but with extra information for left-handed ones. If you are left-handed it may sometimes be helpful to hold the illustration up to a mirror to check what you are doing.

Chapter 1

Equipment and Materials

I have listed the equipment I use for tailoring, some of which you will already have for dressmaking projects. You can tailor quite successfully if you have, for instance, different pins or needles, but I find the items listed make things easier.

Thimbles.

Equipment

I use extra-long extra-fine **pins** for all my sewing; they can be used with most weights of fabric. With a medium-weight tailoring cloth they are perfect, as the points are very sharp and glide through the fabric when pinning on the pattern, and the extra length of the pins enables you to easily pin enough fabric to secure your seams when sewing.

Betweens **needles** are known as tailors' needles. They are noticeably short; some are only about 3.1cm (1¼in) long. A tailor likes to use these needles as the thimble used has no end in it (see below); with this type of short needle, you don't have to bend your finger back as far to push it through as you would

Pins and needles.

with a normal-length needle.

Have a go with these needles before you dismiss them. Many of my students have been initially very way of using needles this small but, after trying them out, have switched to them and won't use anything else.

I use a tailor's **thimble**; this type has no top on it. This is because a tailor doesn't push the needle through with the top of the finger but with the side of it. You push the needle through the cloth using the area close to your nail, thus using the strongest part of the finger.

Many of my students say they can't use a thimble. As soon as the thimble goes onto the middle finger, they automatically use another one for sewing. The way I was taught to get used to sewing with a thimble was to get a big piece of canvas with a couple of layers of padding placed on top of it; I was then shown how to pad stitch. I covered the entire piece of canvas with small stitches all the way across it, forcing myself to use the thimble. If you do this for a couple of hours, using the thimble becomes second nature; I can't sew without one now. If you don't use a

PRICKING YOUR FINGER

Should you be unfortunate enough to get blood on your sewing, whether it is a jacket or anything else, simply get a length of thread (I like to use basting thread), put it into your mouth and moisten it. Now take the thread and rub it onto the blood stain. It has to be saliva; both blood and saliva have enzymes in them and they work together to lift the blood stain from the fabric.

thimble and you do a lot of tailoring, you will get a very sore finger.

Before thimbles were invented, apprentice tailors were encouraged to do a great deal of sewing to make their fingers bleed – without getting any blood on the garment they were creating, of course. The finger would then scab over. After doing this for about six months a callus would form, producing a built-in thimble! This is a very painful way of acquiring a thimble and I definitely wouldn't recommend it.

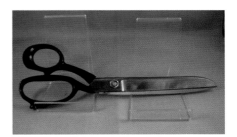

Shears.

In a tailoring workroom you rarely see anything other than large **shears,** somewhere between 20cm (8in) and 30cm (12in) with metal handles. I tend to use 23cm (9in) or 25cm (10in) as my hand aches from the weight of anything bigger. You can get shears up to about 40cm (16in).

I only use my best shears for cutting fabric and I am extremely careful not to drop them.

Use an old pair of shears for cutting

USING TAILOR'S CHALK

Always test the chalk on a spare piece of your fabric before you start, then you can be sure it will brush off without leaving any residue. Always use a sharp piece, so that the line drawn is fine and sharp. Using blunt chalk will give a very thick line and can make markings inaccurate.

You can sharpen your chalk using a pair of scissors (the paper-cutting ones, not the fabric-cutting ones). Be careful if you do this; I only use this method if the chalk sharpener isn't available. A safer way to do this is to use a chalk sharpening box.

pattern paper, otherwise your fabric shears will become blunted and not cut smoothly.

There is the age-old problem of family members borrowing your shears but be very firm about this. I've heard of various methods of controlling such borrowing: the best one I've heard is to use a padlock on the handles!

Tailor's chalk will mark most fabrics. I only use white chalk as there is more chance of it brushing off than if you use coloured chalk. I even use it on white or cream fabrics.

There are many different pens and pencils on the market claiming to do the same job. I only use Hancock's chalk as it contains no wax. Some brands do contain wax and on some fabrics it will stain.

A **chalk sharpening box** has blades set at an angle. To use it you just rub the chalk across the blades on both sides of the chalk; this leaves a very sharp edge, perfect for drawing precise lines on your fabric.

The box in the photo was made for me by a retired tailor, more years ago than I care to admit, and is made from mahogany, but you can get a plastic

Tailor's chalk.

Chalk sharpening box.

Point presser and clapper.

Tailor's ham.

Sleeve roll.

version. The box will give you a beautifully sharp edge to your chalk with little effort.

The **point presser and clapper** is a useful piece of equipment. The clapper or banger is the bottom of the wooden block. When you press a seam or the edge of your jacket you place the clapper on it and it absorbs the steam: this sets the edge immediately, meaning that the fabric won't rise up and give a half-pressed look.

Despite its name you don't have to apply a lot of pressure to make it work.

I find a **tailor's ham** invaluable when making jackets of any sort as it provides a series of curves, some more curvy than others. By using the shape of this ham inside your jacket you can make pressing curves easy without creasing the fabric on either side of the seam you are pressing.

Used in conjunction with the point presser the ham will get a perfect finish for your rounded seams every time you press.

A **sleeve roll** is a useful piece of equipment when pressing sleeve seams open because you don't want to put creases into the sleeve whilst pressing open the sleeve's second seam. I prefer this roll to a sleeve board, as you can accidentally press an impression of the edges of a sleeve board onto the sleeve, leaving creases in it.

It isn't easy to press a sleeve once it's joined up and getting rid of extra creases or impressions just adds to the problem.

Your **iron** needs to become like a friend to you. When tailoring you do need steam and heat to successfully press and shape your jacket. I prefer to use a steam generator iron: this type of iron only produces steam when you press the button, so you will be able to control exactly when and where the steam is applied. This also means that if you don't want to use steam for the seam you are pressing, you don't have to.

An ordinary iron only delivers steam

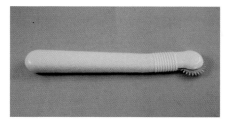

Tracing wheel.

every now and again, so it may well take a bit longer to do the pressing stages.

You can also use a dry iron and a wet cloth but again this takes more time. If you are using a wet cloth, be careful not to get it too wet as water can mark certain cloths.

As my **pressing cloth** I always use a piece of silk organza. This fabric is sheer so you can see through it, enabling you to keep your eye on what you are pressing and you don't press any creases into your sewing by accident. Silk organza is a tough fabric and I promise it won't melt when you use a hot iron on it.

I never finish off the edges of my silk organza pressing cloth, as making a hem or overlocking the edges creates a bulky finish. If you catch this as you are pressing it could leave a mark on the fabric you are pressing. Just trim off the fraying ends as they appear, and after a while the cloth stops fraying. I also wash my cloth when it gets dirty; this does take some of the dressing out of it, but it

prolongs the life of the cloth.

A **tracing wheel** is a useful tool to transfer all the pattern markings to the redrafted dot-and-cross paper pattern once all the fitting stages have been done. Using the wheel means you don't have to lift the pattern out of the way to transfer the markings, which makes it more accurate.

It works best if you put a piece of fabric or a pressing board underneath it. You will have to press quite hard to get the wheel to mark the paper if you just put the pattern onto the work surface. However, be careful if you are using a tracing wheel on a polished table: if you press too hard the spikes on the wheel will damage the surface of the table.

Once you have all the markings traced onto the pattern, you can use a pen or pencil to go over them and mark them clearly.

The **hole punch** is used when hand-finishing. It makes a small hole in the fabric at the end of the buttonhole nearest to the front of the jacket so that the shank of the button can sit comfortably without puckering or distorting the fabric. This punch has several sizes of hole to choose from but you always use the smallest one for buttonholes.

For patterns I use **dot-and-cross paper**, as it is stronger than the traditional

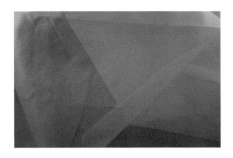

Pressing cloth.

Hole punch.

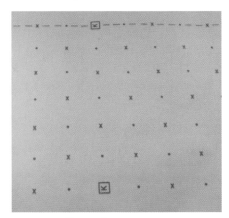

Dot-and-cross paper.

Ruler.

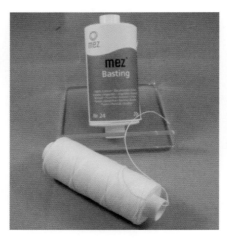
Basting thread.

Beeswax, buttonhole thread and buttonhole gimp.

tissue paper. When I buy a commercial pattern, I trace it out onto the dot-and-cross paper and keep the original pattern for reference only. When making alterations you can stick clear adhesive tape (such as Sellotape) to this paper without creating a problem whereas tissue paper does not take kindly to having lots of tape stuck to it. It can also crease and not sit correctly once the tape is applied; this can cause you to make an inaccurate alteration to your pattern which will then alter the fit of the jacket.

I always have a **ruler** to hand. I use it for altering patterns and for marking cloth using tailor's chalk. I use the one in the photograph, which came from the workroom I was trained in. The end of it has a metal strip, which is a reinforcement to stop the end wearing out. The measurements start right at the end of the ruler, not slightly in, as most of the rulers on the market do.

I'm told that it is more like a ruler used by a carpenter; these are available from DIY stores. I find the 45cm (18in) ruler is more useful than one of 30cm (12in) (too short) or one of 60cm (24in) (too long).

I always use inches for my measurements, but you don't have to if you want to use metric measurements – that's fine. I have put the measurements in both throughout the book, but the conversion isn't exact, so don't start out using one set of measurements and switch halfway through.

When you are tailoring you don't need a **sewing machine** which does

dozens of different stitches. What you do need is a machine which can take heavier-weight fabrics and apply a straight stitch and a basic zigzag stitch.

I love sewing machines, from the basic straight stitch machines to the most complex computerized ones. I'm the first one to jump on a machine and try it out.

Although I have said that you don't need a complicated machine for tailoring, some of the more complex machines are easy to work with and have a lot of time-saving gadgets, for example a thread-cutting button.

This book is not an excuse for buying a

new machine; however, if you get a good deal on one, why not treat yourself!

Basting thread is a special cotton thread made to break easily. It has a slightly rougher texture than a normal thread. This is one item I can't sew without.

Doing tailor tacks is so simple with this thread, as the rough texture of the thread keeps the tailor tack in place.

I also use this thread when putting in temporary basting stitches which hold layers of fabrics together whilst more permanent stitches are put in place. Basting thread is perfect when pulling out the basting stiches right at the end of the making-up process. Should it get caught when you are pulling it out, it snaps, unlike ordinary thread which would cut into the fabric.

I use **beeswax** to strengthen the thread when I'm hand-working buttonholes. You pull the thread through the wax, then take it to the iron. Make sure you have a piece of scrap fabric on the ironing board. Place the thread onto the scrap fabric and fold the fabric over, place the hot iron gently on top and then pull the thread through. This will remove any excess wax before you start the buttonhole. The wax will then not get on to the ironing board or the iron and then transfer to your jacket when you press it. This process leaves enough wax on the thread to strengthen it but not enough to stain the front when you press the finished buttonhole.

The piece of beeswax you can see in the photograph was given to me by my grandfather when I started tailoring. He used to work in the shoe industry and used this piece of wax in his work.

You can buy special heavyweight thread to work buttonholes with: in the trade it's known as **buttonhole twist**. If you can't get hold of this thread, then use a topstitching thread (a slightly thicker thread) which is readily available in most stores where you buy ordinary cotton threads. There is a good choice of colours in topstitching thread, which is a good thing as women's jackets come in a bigger variety of colours than men's. Traditional buttonhole thread comes in an very limited choice of colours.

Buttonhole gimp is a thick thread which is placed onto the edge of the buttonhole and the buttonhole stitch is then worked over it. This gives a rounded, slightly padded shape to the edge of your buttonhole.

The thread is made up of several core threads, with an outside lighter thread wrapped around the core. It has almost a wire-like feel to it. If you can't get hold of any gimp, you can use several strands of the topstitching thread instead; these strands can be waxed to make them stronger.

Materials

Most people think that when you sew anything you just need the fabric and perhaps a lining, if needed.

The list of fabrics here looks like quite a long one. This is an extra expense, on top of your fabric and lining, so why are they all necessary?

Creating a jacket is not like sewing anything else. You need some support inside the jacket to help to keep its

Fabrics for inside the jacket.

shape and this is done by a variety of materials. The main canvasses will be shaped for what is known as the T-zone. Basically, this supports the front of the jacket, the front edge where the buttonholes will be, and up through the lapels and into the collar. It also supports the sleeves into the armhole.

The under collar will need its own interfacing to support the top collar as well. I will be explaining how to cut and use these different interfacings as we go along.

The following are the fabrics I have used whilst making the jacket featured.

Fabric for the jacket

Traditional tailoring is time-consuming as there is a lot of hand-stitching to do: I always use a mediumweight pure wool fabric. It's not worth doing this method on a cheap fabric.

I expect my jackets to last for as long as possible – at least ten years, maybe twenty.

This is possible, providing you don't change shape, of course. A cheap, polyester fabric will start looking out of shape within a few wearings of the jacket.

I like to use an acetate **lining** if possible. I'm a big fan of patterned lining but if I can't get that, then a satin lining always looks beautiful.

Jacket lining is usually a bit heavier than the lining you would use in dressmaking.

You can always decorate the lining yourself if you can't get a patterned one you like. (*See* Chapter 5 for details.)

For a woman's jacket I use a **lightweight tailoring canvas**. You can get heavier weights than I use but I find that the wearers usually prefer the jacket not to be too stiff and heavy. This fabric will form the base layer of interfacing for the T-zone.

A **heavy chest canvas** is used for the base of the chest piece or plastron (see Chapter 7 for details). This canvas will spring back to shape if it's squashed whilst you are wearing the jacket; for instance, if you put a handbag on your shoulder or put on a seat belt in the car.

A soft **domette** is used for the top part of the chest piece or plastron. This is to add a layer of padding to the plastron and to stop the rougher texture of the chest canvas from coming through to the lining.

I like to use a lining for my pocket bags, but you can use a **cotton pocketing** (the best-known variety of which is called silesia) for this. It is quite tightly woven and is therefore stronger and longer-lasting than ordinary lining.

Usually I only put tissues into my jacket pockets. If you are intending to use them for other, heavier things or more often, then the cotton pocketing would definitely be preferable to ordinary lining.

Duck linen is a lighter-weight canvas I like to use for the collar of a lady's jacket as traditional collar canvas can be a bit too stiff.

This interfacing is hand-padded to the under collar to create the shape; the top collar then becomes just a decoration to cover up the workings underneath.

I use a pure **cotton lawn** to give some support to the lapel whilst pad stitching. The nature of the cutting of a jacket means that the main fabric and the canvas are slightly off-grain where the break line is positioned. If the break line were cut on the straight grain, the front edge would be off-grain, causing a lot of problems with the hang of the jacket.

By cutting this piece of fabric on the straight grain, it stops the main fabric

and the canvas from stretching out too much, whilst still allowing for the shaping of the lapel.

Volume fleece is a wadding fabric used in the head of the sleeve to pad out the gap between the head of the sleeve and the armhole of the jacket, giving a generous, rounded appearance to the crown of the sleeve.

In traditional tailoring a sleeve head is usually used but I find that they can prove a bit bulky for ladies' tailoring. I prefer how the volume fleece creates a padded roll for the shoulder pads to sit on but, depending on the style, you could use a sleeve head as well or

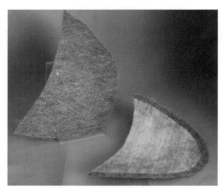
Shoulder pads.

instead of the volume fleece.

I use an off-grain **edge tape** for the edges of the jacket: this is a fusible tape cut at about 13 degrees off straight grain.

This degree of stretch enables you to go around a shaped edge but still provides the stability of a stay tape.

I use this tape on the front edge of the jacket and then it is hand-stitched to the canvas.

Traditionally a non-fusible wide linen stay tape is hand-stitched to the edge, but again I find this makes a bulky edge, far too heavy for a woman's jacket.

I use felt **shoulder pads** in my jackets. These pads don't compress down when you stitch them in, unlike the foam ones. Nor do they disintegrate over time like the foam pads tend to do. They are not too big and bulky, perfect for ladies' tailoring.

Hand Stitches

When I'm hand-stitching anything, I always use thread which is cut the length of my arm. When this length is threaded through the needle it means

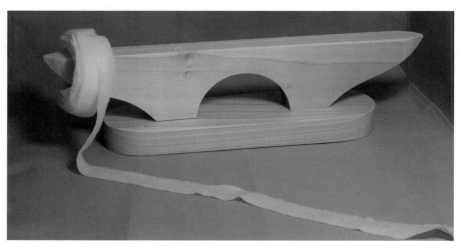
Edge tape.

Slip stitching a hem, step 1.

Slip stitching a hem, step 2.

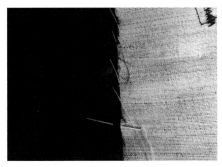

Slip stitch for other areas.

Basting.

that you will always be able to pull the thread straight through in one movement and not have to go back and tug the last bit of thread through.

Some of my students like to cut exceptionally long lengths of thread so they won't have to thread the needle twice. This wastes a lot of time when you are hand-stitching, and the thread may break or get twisted as you stitch.

I've used a white thread in the following photographs where appropriate, so you can see the stitches.

I use **slip stitch** for hems or any invisible stitching inside the jacket. This stitch can be done in two ways, depending on which part of the jacket you are stitching. For the hemline you fold back the edge of the hem. If you are stitching any other part of the jacket, you keep the edges flat and sew over them.

To slip stitch a hem, first baste the hemline in place. Turn back about 6mm (¼in) of the hem, leaving you with a fold near the edge of the hem.

Then, using a single thread of the cotton you are using to sew the jacket, pick up a single thread of fabric from the jacket and a stitch from the folded hem. The stitches need to be about 1.3mm (½in) apart and are worked towards you.

If you take a small enough stitch in the main fabric, the hemming will be invisible on the right side. Once you have completed the stitching, fold the hem back up. Your stitching will then be underneath the hem and it will be almost impossible to catch and pull it.

To slip stitch areas other than a hem, again use the cotton being used for the main fabric. Slip the needle under the edge to be fastened.

Bring the needle over the edge of the seamline and take a stitch into the fabric you are fastening it to, and back into the seamline.

The stitches can be quite large, about 2cm (¾in). For the picture I have used a white thread so that it is easier to see the

stitches.

Make sure that you only stitch through the two layers of fabric you are fastening; don't go through to the right side of the fabric.

As with the previous version of this stitch it is worked towards you.

Basting is the tailor's word for tacking. Most basting stitches are only temporary, put in to hold some part of the jacket whilst you put more

Thread tracing.

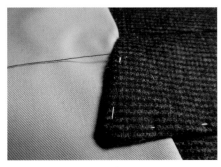

Prick stitch, step 1.

Prick stitch, step 2.

permanent stitches in place.

Basting stitches are usually quite large, up to 7cm (3in) long but dipping through the layers for a much shorter distance, all using a single thread. I always use a knot at the end of the thread; it is easier to pull out basting if you can pull the knot.

Some of the basting threads do stay in the jacket permanently; they will be inside the jacket, so no one will be able to see them.

When I get to the end of the row of basting, I put in a back stitch to secure the end and then, using my thumbnail on the cotton, just snap it off: it's much

Felling.

quicker than using scissors. This trick only works with basting thread; please don't try it on ordinary thread as you will probably end up cutting into the cloth or ruining your nails.

Thread tracing It is similar to basting but the surface stitches are smaller, about 2.5cm (1in), and the pick-up stitches are considerably smaller. A thread-traced line should look like an almost continuous length of thread. Thread tracing is usually used to mark an area ready for either pressing or stitching.

Prick stitching is a topstitch used on pockets or to hold the edge of the jacket. It is worked from right to left (but from left to right if you are left-handed). Use a single thread of ordinary cotton (although you can use a thicker, topstitching thread to give a more prominent stitch) and bring the needle to the right side of the jacket.

Now do a tiny backstitch, usually over a couple of threads. Come out of the cloth about 6mm (¼in) further along the piece. By using such a small stitch, you

will only see a tiny dot of a stitch forming on the right side, hence the name prick stitch.

If you are topstitching the edges of a jacket, you can work either directly on the edge of the cloth or 6mm (¼in) in from the edge: this all depends on the effect you wish to create. The former makes the stitching almost invisible; the latter makes it more decorative.

Felling is used to secure the lining hem of the jacket or sleeve. Like slip stitching it can be worked on the edge of the fabric or with the fabric folded back. If you do it with the edge folded back the stitches will be invisible once the edge is put back into its finished position.

This stitch is worked from right to left (or the reverse if you are left-handed). Again, you need a single thread to work this stitch.

Fold back the hemline by putting your needle about halfway between the folded edge and the basting line. You can then separate the two layers of the folded hem.

Pull the top layer up and backwards to

Pad stitching the plastron, step 1.

Pad stitching the plastron, step 2.

reveal a fold: this is where you will stitch.

Take a small amount of the cloth from the main fabric, making sure you are not going through to the right side of the jacket, then a small amount from the folded-back edge.

Once you have stitched the hem, smooth the top layer back down to cover the stitches.

The stitch length is a maximum of 6mm (¼in). These stitches are permanent and need to be very neat.

You can work this stitch in exactly the same way but not folding back the hemline, just using the folded edge of the hemline instead. I use the stitch this way when felling the edge of the lining at the bottom of the sleeve, stitching the lining for the armhole into place and finishing the edges of the welt pocket.

Pad stitching is a very clever stitch and can be sewn in two different ways. Whichever method you use, the stitch is worked in the same way, just held differently.

The first method is to use it flat on a table to hold layers of cloth together. (I use this for the layers of the plastron.) You are stitching three layers together, so keeping everything flat on the table will stop the layers moving whilst you are stitching.

I find it quicker if you use the table to bounce the needle off as you take a stitch. Be careful when doing this, as the needle pricks will mark the table below. Don't do it if you are working on your polished dining table (I use a cutting table with a plywood finish to it).

Place the layers needing to be sewn on a table. I use a single thread of basting

Pad stitching for shaping, step 1.

Pad stitching for plastron, step 3.

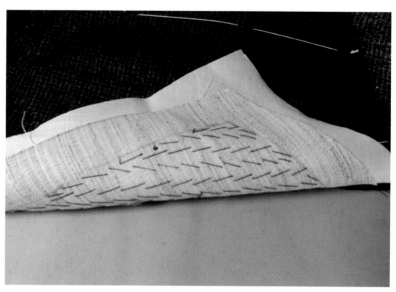

Pad stitching for shaping, step 2.

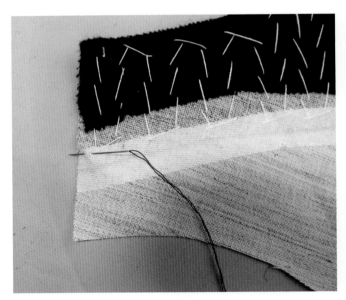

Herringbone stitch, step 1.

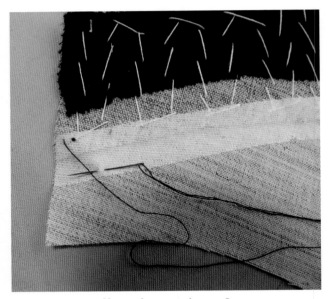

Herringbone stitch, step 2.

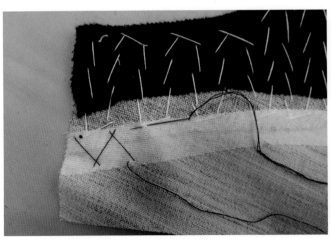

Herringbone stitch, step 3.

thread to sew with. Start at the top of the piece, near to the left-hand side. Work a small running stitch from right to left (but the reverse if you are left-handed).

Make sure you are going through all three layers with your stitch, although at the bottom of the plastron you will only be going through two layers of fabric due to the layering of the pieces.

Don't lift the pieces off the table as you stitch: this could distort the layers.

Come down below the first stitch by about 1.5cm (⅝in) and work another stitch in the same direction as the first one.

Continue to stitch in this manner until you reach the bottom of the piece.

Now work a second row of stitching about 1.3cm (½in) away from the first row, this time placing the stitches so that the new stitch is level with the middle of the stitches on the first row.

Work from the bottom up towards the top of the plastron. By working in this way, it means you don't have to break the thread at the end of each row. The rows of stitching should look like the backbone of a herring.

Continue to work up and down the piece, exactly as the first two rows, covering the rest of the fabric.

You can also use pad stitching for shaping the lapels and collar.

Use the thread which matches the jacket fabric to work this version.

The stitches are worked in the same way as for the plastron but they are much smaller, 1cm (⅜in), and the rows are only 1cm (⅜in) apart. As you sew these stitches you fold the fabric over: this puts the shape into the piece.

As you sew out towards the edge, move the fold of the piece with you.

You should always be working on the top of the fold.

By moving the fold with you as you go, you shorten the main fabric, which means the canvas and cotton lawn have further to travel.

When you get to the edge, you shouldn't be able to lay the lapel flat.

Herringbone stitch is used in several places around the jacket, particularly on the inside where the lining and the facing meet at the front of the jacket.

If you work the stitch over the raw edge, you don't have to turn in the edge, which would make a bulky finish.

It is also used to hold the front edge of the shoulder pad in place and on the canvasses when securing the tape at the bottom of the plastron.

Wherever you are using this stitch

there will be two edges to secure. The photos show the bottom edge of the canvas.

Using a single thread, make a running stitch onto the top edge of the tape, slightly in from the edge.

Put another running stitch into the bottom edge of the tape slightly to the right-hand side of the first stitch, just inside the bottom edge. Then return to the top of the tape and do the same as before.

As you work backwards and forwards from left to right the threads should cross over; this looks like a herring's bones, hence the name. If you are left-handed you will find it easier to work in the opposite direction.

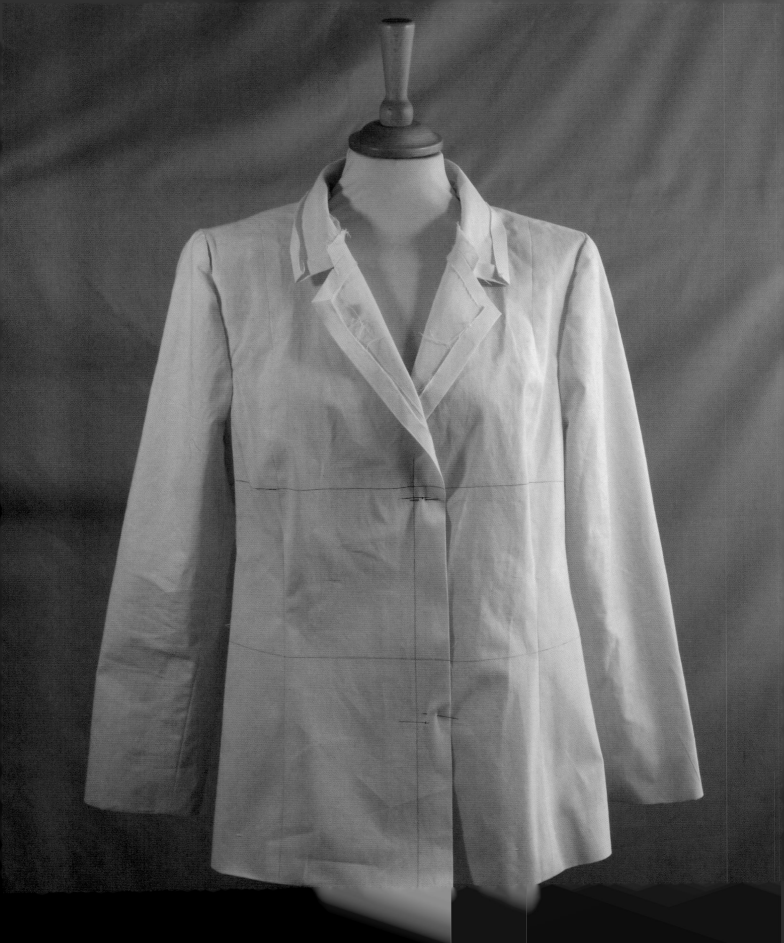

Chapter 2

Choosing the Pattern and Fitting with the Toile

Patterns fascinate me, in that we go from a flat pattern drawn out on a piece of paper to a three-dimensional garment made in fabric. I quite often lay out the pattern so that the pieces which go together in the final garment are side by side. By doing this you can see where all the shaping is. If you look at the pieces you will find shapes which look like darts taken out of the pieces to form the shaping for bust, waist and hips to start with and then a whole series of different shapes for style lines.

I'm not a fan of drafting patterns from scratch: the whole process can be quite boring if you don't like figures. This doesn't mean I can't do it but, in my opinion, the pattern companies have far more experience of doing it and use qualified pattern drafters and very accurate, complex computer systems to produce the patterns. I tend to use a commercial base pattern and adapt it for my own purpose.

There is nothing wrong with using your own pattern if you have gone to the trouble of drafting it. When you draft your own pattern, it will still need to be tried out in toile form (a mock-up of the garment) and adjusted to your own personal shape. No amount of measurement can take into account all our personal nooks and crannies. If we were all square blocks measurements would be easier to take and patterns easier to draft; however, we would all look very strange.

I have a lot of pattern drafting books, some dating back to the turn of the

twentieth century, and I love to see how the patterns were drafted then. The basic block pattern is more or less the same. Through all the books I have, you can see the way the basic pattern was adapted to the styles which were fashionable at the time of the book going to print. It's this side of pattern drafting which I find the most interesting.

We are lucky to have so many beautiful patterns available to us today. Sometimes the choice can be quite confusing. I like to look for a princess-line pattern for jackets: the seams on the front and back of the jacket enable you to expand or take in the shape as much as you need. This is a perfect solution for anyone who has, for instance, a larger bust than the normal B cup the patterns allow for. The pattern I'm using for this book has the princess-line seams at front and back but also has a side body panel, giving you more seams to use for alterations. On this pattern there is no side seam.

I only use the pattern for the basic shapes for the outside of the jacket. I ignore all the lining, pockets and interfacing pieces. I'm going to show you throughout the book the easy way to cut these pieces and guarantee that they will fit whatever shape you are.

Check the measurements of the jacket with the back of the pattern before you start. These measurements are a standard size.

Now I know that nobody is a standard size. So, why bother with them? Think of these measurements as a starting point.

The pattern companies can't possibly cater for all the sizes and shapes out there. Be honest with yourself when you are doing these measurements. Your waist, for instance, may be bigger than you would like it to be – I think most of us have that problem – but if you want this jacket to fit don't imagine you are smaller than the tape measure says.

You may find that you are cutting a bigger size than you would buy in the shops: so be it. Shops do sell what is known in the trade as flattering sizes, so your pattern may well be a bigger size than you are used to.

When you make for yourself it doesn't matter what size you are; you don't put a size label into handmade clothes. It will be a you size.

Amending the Pattern

There are a couple of things that I alter on a commercial pattern. The first is the sleeve. I always **cut the sleeve one size larger** than the pattern I'm cutting. This is to allow extra fullness in the sleeve head.

I know you are all shouting 'No, not more fullness!'. On the toile you will struggle to get this in without a couple of small pleats but once you try to get the sleeve into the armhole using a lovely soft wool fabric the extra fullness means you won't finish up with a tight or flat sleeve head.

The other alteration I do is to **reposition the break line:** this is the line where the front folds back to create the

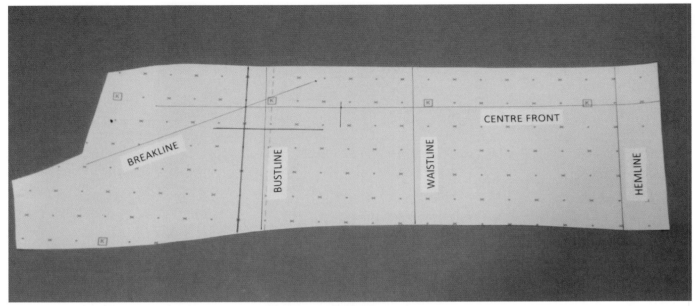

Repositioning the break line.

lapel.

The break line on the patterns always seem to be positioned so it runs in front of the seam allowance at the neck edge. If you use this line, when you put your collar on the roll line the under collar doesn't match up with the break line. This is extremely easy to correct.

You will find a dot on the pattern at the start of this line, just above the top button mark. This dot is known as the break point: it's the point at which the front makes a break from being the front and becomes the lapel.

This is your starting point. The end of the break line should be 1.5 (⅝in) inside the neck edge of the jacket. If you mark it this way the roll line of the collar will be a continuation of the break line.

I like to make the toile with no **shaping at the bottom of the front edge**. The front edge is square with the hemline and bottom of the pattern. The pattern I am using has this already on it, but if yours doesn't it is easy to adapt it.

Simply draw a straight line from the

front edge downwards until it's level with the bottom of the jacket.

I do this so I can make my own mind up about the shaping. If you have a round bottom to your pattern to start with, you can't change your mind when you get to shaping the front edges. I will be showing you how to draw in the front edge later in the book.

I now transfer the tissue paper pattern to dot-and-cross paper. This paper is much stronger than the tissue, so you can make as many alterations as you need without tearing it.

Make sure when you transfer the pattern that you get the straight grain line on the pattern pieces, running along the lines of the dots and crosses.

You can transfer all the lines on the pattern using a tracing wheel. Place the dot-and-cross paper down on to the table with the tissue pattern on top. You will have to press quite firmly to make the teeth marks of the wheel come through to the dot-and-cross paper.

I like to put a spare piece of cloth

underneath the pattern: this gives a soft surface, making it easier to see the marks when you wheel along. A pressing board is a good alternative if you have one.

Once you have traced the whole pattern through to the dot-and-cross paper, mark in all the lines with a pencil. The original pattern can now be put away and you can work on the dot-and-cross paper version.

This gives you a safety net just in case the alterations go very wrong: you can always go back to the original pattern at any time. Also, you can easily stick as much adhesive tape as you like to this paper without distorting it.

Making the Toile

Choosing the pattern and the fabric is the start of a great adventure and I love this stage.

The toile making and fitting are the most important and yet the most boring. If you are anything like me, you will

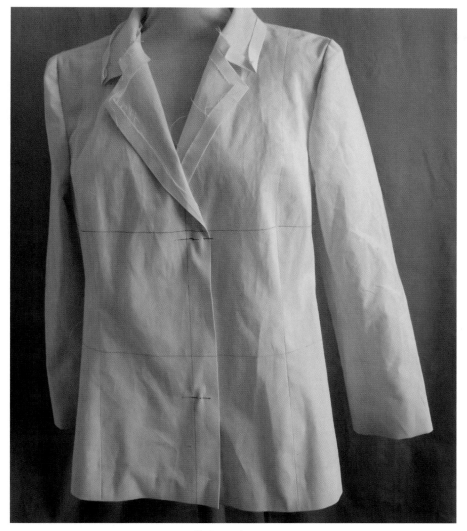

Toile markings.

cared less.

It's as we get a little older and wiser that we realize that fitting is important to the look of the garment.

In a gentlemen's tailoring workroom, they mark the jacket pieces in the cloth using chalk and then cut out. They include inlays (variable seam allowances), which allow for some alterations in the jacket.

Ladies' jackets are a little bit different. We have more curves to go around, so when I'm making a jacket, I like to make a toile to get it right. I always use calico for this.

It is not necessary to make a completely finished jacket for the toile.

When buying calico, look for one that has the same weight and feel (heft) as your main fabric; I usually use one of medium weight. Bleached calico tends to be slightly softer than unbleached.

Cutting and marking

Lay out the pattern pieces on the calico, just as you would lay them out on the main fabric, paying particular attention to the straight grain of the cloth. Cut carefully round.

You don't need to finish off the edges; I just crease the hem and outside edges with the iron.

Note: I don't cut the vent for the sleeve on a toile, as it just flaps about whilst fitting. Instead, fold the vent in on the pattern by a seam allowance (usually 1.5cm or ⅝in) away from the finished fold line along the vent. Cut the sleeve with a straight seam finish, no vent, just for the toile.

Then use a pen or pencil to mark the **essential lines** on the calico, thus making the lines very visible when you are fitting the jacket to the person who is going to be wearing it.

To make sure the lines are in the same place on each side of the pattern, first

want to jump straight into cutting your beautiful fabric. *Don't.*

Think of it like this: once you have done all this preparation you will have a jacket pattern that fits you perfectly.

This pattern can then be used time and time again. We all have figure variations, and in all the time I've been making and fitting jackets, I've never come across the perfect standard-size pattern-shaped person.

I've had lots of ladies who think they are, until I start to fit them properly and then they realize how important fitting clothes is.

I also meet many ladies who say, 'I used to be a standard size 12 or 14 when I was younger'. I have a theory about this: when I was younger, I used to just make up a standard size and I can't remember doing any fittings at all, apart from length. As long as it was the latest fashion and I could wear it the same night I started to sew it; I couldn't have

mark the line on the top piece of calico. When you have that in the right place, crease the two layers of fabric along the line you have just marked. Now use this line to mark in the underneath layer of fabric.

These markings need to be on the *right* side of the calico when you are making the toile up.

As you can see from the picture there are lots of marks on the toile to help get everything in the correct place. Start with the following lines on both left and right sides of your toile.

The **bustline, waistline** and **hemline** are marked so you can check that the jacket is level all round.

The two centre front panels are laid one over the other to fasten the toile whilst fitting it, so the **centre front line** is especially important.

The **break line** (roll line for the lapel) is marked so that you can check that the lapel is in the correct position for the person wearing it by folding the toile along this line.

By marking in the **top and bottom button positions**, you are able to see if they are in the correct position for the person wearing the jacket. If you make any alterations to the length of the jacket you may need to consider where the buttons are positioned.

Now let's turn to the other marks. When you have cut the pattern pieces out, you will need some **balance marks** to make the making-up process easier. I don't use all the marks on the pattern; manufacturers tend to put lots on, which can be confusing. The marks I use are listed below.

On the centre front panel, mark the **dot at the top of the lapel**. It's the place where the lapel stops and the collar starts. Every piece of the pattern which forms the collar and the lapel will have this dot marked on it; I like to call it the magic dot.

On the under collar, mark the **dot for the notched collar.** This is 1.5cm (⅝in) away from the neck edge and the same distance from the side edge of the collar. This is an important dot when you are making up the jacket: everything for the collar application either starts or finishes at this dot.

On the side body panel, mark the **underarm dot**, which is where the sleeve will match. If you are using a pattern with an underarm seam, this dot is not necessary and won't be marked on the pattern. You can match the under sleeve dot to the side seam instead.

On the upper sleeve, mark the **dot at the top of the sleeve** so that you can position the sleeve against the shoulder seam.

On the under sleeve, mark the **dot in the middle of the underarm**. This dot matches to the dot on the side body or the side seam when positioning the sleeve.

When you are sewing the pieces together, try to be as accurate as possible. Take your time to get the seam allowances to the right size. Very often in my workroom I've heard someone say, 'It's only a toile', but this is the garment you are using to get a perfect fit for your beautiful jacket, so take your time and get it right.

I use a bigger machine stitch when making a toile, 3.5 instead of 2.5. Calico will take this longer stitch without puckering, which makes it quicker to sew the seams.

Sewing the toile

1. Sewing the vertical jacket seams
Sew together all the body panels of the jacket, pressing the seams open as you go. Make sure all your pencil markings are on the outside: this will make the fitting much easier.

Whilst the jacket is still fairly flat, press in the hem allowance along the bottom. If you have marked and sewn this accurately there should be a continuous pencil line running round the bottom of the jacket for you to follow.

Note: When pressing calico, use heat only: steam could cause shrinkage.

I like to do as many processes as I can whilst the piece is flat. Once you join the shoulder seams it becomes a three-dimensional shape, which makes it a lot more difficult to handle.

This is the point at which you can see

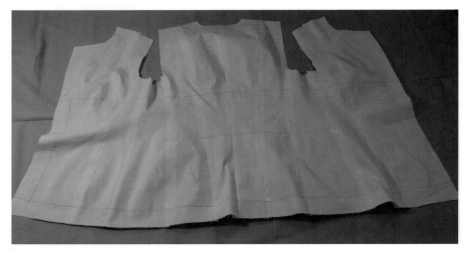

Toile, step 1, jacket seams.

all the shaping allowed on the pattern. As you can see from the photograph, it is impossible for you to lay the toile out completely flat. You can already see the shaping for the bustline, waistline and so on.

2. Shoulder seams

Once all the body pieces are joined together, stitch the shoulder seams and press open. Now you can see the jacket in its three-dimensional shape, looking something like it will when it is finished.

3. Under collar

Sew the seam at the centre back of the under collar, then press it open. Whilst you are at the ironing board, press in the seam allowances along the sides and back edge of the collar.

4. Attaching the under collar

Match the dot at the front of the collar to the dot at the start of the lapel on the jacket front. You will have to clip the neck edge of the jacket to enable this to fit.

If you look at the task in hand, it looks

almost impossible to do. The collar is almost a straight line with a bit of a kink at the end whereas the neckline of the jacket is a rounded shape with a straight bit on each end.

Don't despair. If you clip into the neckline at the point where it reaches the break line on the pattern, this will enable you to pin the collar so that it goes up to the break line on the straight side. Then you will be able to swing the collar around the corner.

You will then have to snip around the neck edge of the collar to make it fit. As long as you don't snip beyond the 1.5cm (⅝in) stitching line, you can put as many snips into the neckline as are

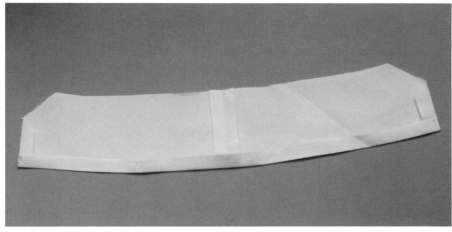

Toile, step 3, under collar.

EASING THE COLLAR

When you are machining the seam, concentrate on keeping just the next 5cm (2in) straight and the underneath fabric flat. You won't be able to lay the whole of the collar flat before you start. This is a tricky task but take your time.

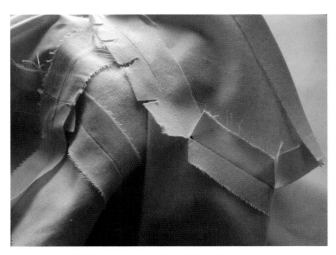

Toile, step 4, attaching the under collar.

Toile, step 5, long sleeve seam.

necessary to make the collar fit the neckline.

Sew from the magic dot on one side of the under collar around the back neck to the magic dot on the other side of the collar.

When you are stitching, keep an eye on the edges of the seam, as the edges have a tendency to try to come apart. This is due to the very different shapes you are trying to stitch together. This is a common problem people have with collars; if you let the edges part, it makes the seam impossible to stitch without getting pleats in it.

Press the seam open; I like to use the tailor's ham to help with this process. You may need to snip again to make the seam lie flat.

You don't need the top collar for this fitting.

5. Sleeves

Sew up the long sleeve seam (hindarm seam) first. (When making the sleeve up with the vent in place, the short seam will be stitched first.)

For the toile it is easier to press the long seam before you join the sleeve into a cylinder.

Press the seam open; again, you may find the tailor's ham useful.

Whilst you are at the iron, crease in the hemline of the sleeve: it's much easier to do whilst the sleeve is still almost flat.

Then stitch the short seam (forearm seam). Press this open using a sleeve roll.

Now sew a row of basting around the crown (top) of the sleeve.

If your machine has a basting stitch on it, use that; if not, just put the machine up to the longest stitch it will do.

You need to machine from the right side of the sleeve and take a slightly bigger seam than the one allowed on the pattern.

This is because when you pull the

threads up to take in the fullness, you will be able to see a flat surface just beyond the stitching.

When you take a proper seam allowance when putting the sleeve into

position, you will be stitching on this flat area. This makes sleeve insertion much easier.

When you are ready to insert the sleeve, pull up the basting stitches from

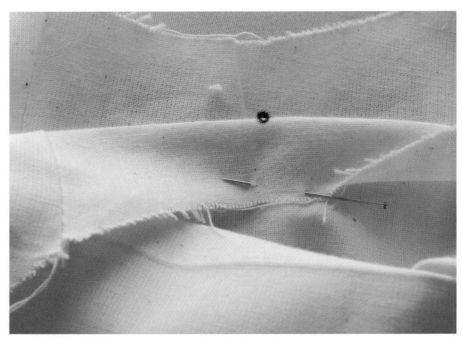

Toile, step 6, inserting the sleeve into the armhole.

Toile, step 7, pressing in the front edge and hemline.

the wrong side of the fabric. The stitches should pull up easily from this side.

6. Inserting the sleeve into the armhole

Make sure you match the dots on the sleeve to the shoulder seam and the dot in the middle of the side body or side seam first.

Then pin the rest of the sleeve into place.

Don't worry if you have a couple of small pleats at the top or crown of the sleeve. It is difficult to put a smooth sleeve head into calico. It will be much easier in your woollen fabric.

Once the sleeve is in the armhole, you can remove the row of basting; this is easier if you pull the threads on the wrong side of the stitching.

7. Pressing in the seam allowances

There is no need to put the front facing onto the jacket for a toile fitting, but you will need to press in the seam allowance along the front edge, up to the dot at the start of the notched collar. These seams should stay in place just by pressing them. Be accurate with the measuring of this allowance.

The hemline needs to be pressed in place as well.

You may need to baste the hemline on the jacket and the sleeves into place to stop them falling down during fitting. If you think you will be altering the length of the jacket or sleeves, you could just pin them, making it easier to alter, but I prefer to baste it into place as it's more secure.

8. Shoulder pad

If you are intending to use a shoulder pad in your final jacket, you will need to put a pad into the toile. I don't usually go to the trouble of basting it in place; I just slip it into the shoulder area once the jacket is on the figure. You may need to reposition it or you may decide you don't want it at all; this is much easier to do if it's loose.

Fitting the Toile

There is no easy way to say this, but you can't fit yourself. You will have to find a friend to do the pinning. Many ladies say that they try to persuade their husbands to do the fitting and some even manage to do it quite successfully but whoever you persuade to help you, the chances are they won't be a sewer. You will need to guide them as to the alterations needed. You must learn to 'read' what the toile is saying. This expression sounds a bit weird, but if you can tell someone what is wrong, they can usually pin it out and you should be able transfer it to the pattern.

If you are not sure what's wrong with the fitting, get your helper to pinch out the problem in different directions. Watch what happens to the toile when they do this. The jacket will just drop into position when you get it right. Remember, we all have figure variations.

When you put the toile on for the fitting, make sure that you accurately pin the centre front lines one over the other, matching the top button position and pinning down to the bottom button. If the toile has come out too small, place the lines as near as possible one over the other and measure the difference. Write down this measurement, as you will never remember it once you have done the rest of the fitting.

Slip the shoulder pad in place. Before you start to look at the fit of the jacket, move around as if you were wearing the finished jacket. Check to see how it feels. Does one part of it feel too loose or too tight? Does it feel comfortable to do what you need to do whilst wearing the jacket? I repeat this process once I've done all the fittings; this will check that the fitting hasn't been overdone.

Toiles are never the most flattering garment you will wear, so try to look at the fitting and style of the jacket, ignoring the fabric.

I have never come across anyone who wanted to make a jacket out of calico.

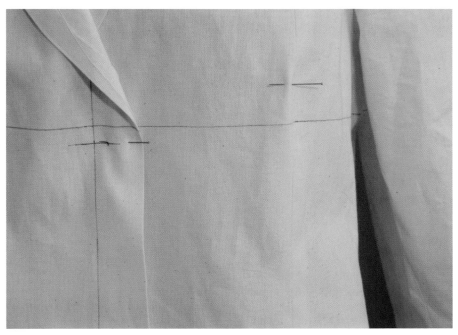

Fitting, step 1, levels.

1. Levels

Look at the levels – bustline, waistline and hemline. Are they in the correct place for your figure?

If not, put a pin horizontally where these positions should be. Check that they are level all the way around the body. If necessary, repeat this process.

Check that the shoulder and side seams are in the correct place. Again, use a pin parallel to the seam to indicate where they should be on you.

2. Excess fabric in seams

Now look to see if there is any excess fabric which can be taken in using the seams.

Using the seams for taking in excess fabric is much easier than pinning out where there isn't a seam. Pin the excess out so you have equal amounts of fabric either side of the seam. If, as in the photo, you are taking excess from the two side body seams, try to pin the excess out equally on both seams.

If there is an obvious difference on each side of the body (which does happen), pin out what you can see, and you will have to do two separate alterations to the pattern.

3. Excess fabric not in seams

Sometimes it is impossible to get rid of all the excess fabric using the seams. So the next step is to check to see if there is any excess fabric folding outwards where there aren't any seams, for example if there is pleating on the back

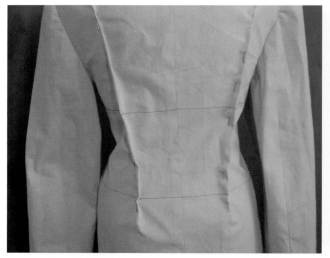

Fitting, step 2, excess fabric in seams.

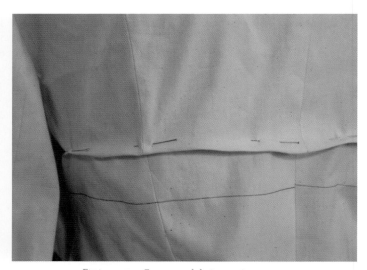

Fitting, step 3, excess fabric not in seams.

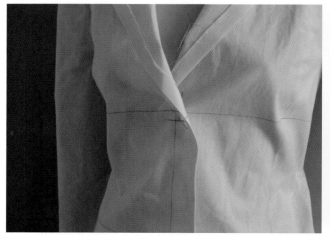

Fitting, step 4, fabric pulling tight.

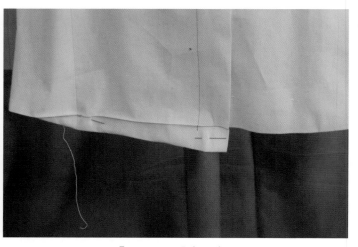

Fitting, step 5, lengths.

of the jacket due to a sway back. Get your friend to pin out this fabric wherever it may be and in whatever direction makes the jacket sit properly on your body. The pins may need to be repositioned several times to get the jacket hanging correctly.

4. Fabric pulling tight

Next, look for anything which may be pulling tight and calculate how much extra fabric you need to add to make it fit.

If, for instance, the front is pulling tight, look to see if the princess-line seam is in the correct place. If it isn't, measure how much you need to move it to make it sit in the right position.

This is more difficult than taking excess fabric in, but it certainly validates making the voile.

5. Lengths

Next, look at the length of the jacket and the sleeves.

You don't have to stick to what the pattern is suggesting; you may want to make one or both slightly longer or shorter.

When you are making up your mind about these lengths, bear in mind your body shape and the proportions of the finished jacket. Cutting a jacket too short, for instance, can make you look really square, where cutting it a bit longer would be more flattering.

If you are altering the length, have a look where the bottom button is positioned; you may need to move it.

Remove a small section of the basting to help you roll down the jacket to check the length.

Once you have decided on the length, you can then remove the rest of the basting and let the rest of the hem down.

Check that the jacket is level all round.

Now check the sleeve length. There are all sorts of views as to the correct place for the sleeve to finish. I prefer to ask the person who will be wearing the garment as to where they feel comfortable for the sleeve to finish.

I, for instance, have longer arms than the average person; if I buy anything in a shop, the sleeves are always about 2.5cm (1in) too short for me. When I make a jacket, I like my sleeves to be slightly longer than most people.

Play around with the sleeves until you are happy with the length. Check that both sleeves need adjusting to the same length: in some cases, your arms could be different lengths.

6. Collar

Look at the collar to see if it's in the right place for you. Check to see if there are any wrinkles around the edge of it and that the roll line is in the right place. If not, re-pin it to the correct position and

mark it on the pattern.

7. Marking the pocket position

It is quite easy at this stage to work out where you would like the pocket to be positioned. There will be a line marked on the pattern, but it might not be in the right place for you.

To get the pocket placement right, simply put your hands up to the front of the jacket as if you were going to put something into the pocket. Don't think about it, just put your hands where it feels comfortable.

Get your helper to mark with pins where your hands are positioned. Take the toile off and mark the position with a horizontal pencil line. The front of the pocket should be marked with a vertical line going through the first line, approx. 2.5cm (1in) in front of the princess-line seam.

Now try the toile on again and test again by putting your hands into your pretend pockets. If you are putting your hands into the position marked, you have the pocket marked correctly; if not, try marking it again. You can vary the pockets by marking a straight or slanted line, whichever you are happiest with.

By doing the positioning at this point, you can transfer the pocket position to the pattern and you will never need to work it out again.

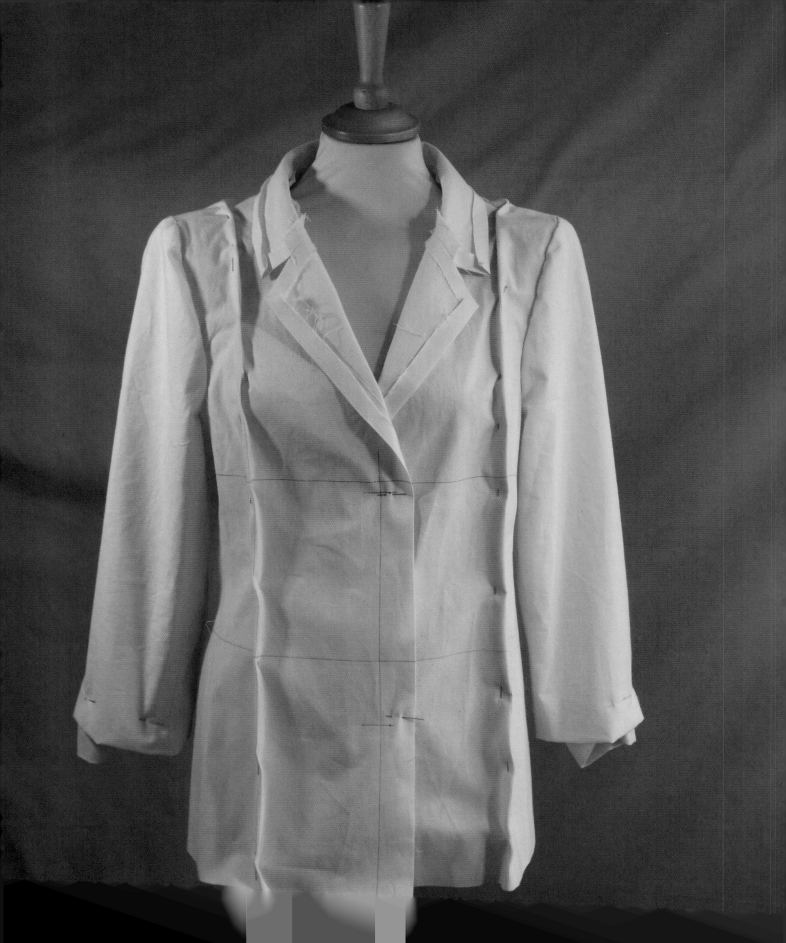

Chapter 3

Pattern Alterations

There are so many possible alterations that I could fill another book about just that subject, so I'm going to show you how to solve some of the most common problems that I have come across in my workroom.

When working on alterations you need to make sure you do what's needed while keeping the pattern as near to the original shape as possible.

Remember, when you alter one piece you need to bear in mind which other pieces it will be stitched to.

I spend lots of time when I do alterations trying the altered pattern piece against the one it's going to fit to. It's much easier to alter a piece of paper than trying to alter the fabric once it's cut. This process is called 'truing' the pattern. The instructions for truing the pattern are at the end of the chapter.

Concentrate on completing one alteration at a time, even if another is on the same pattern piece. It's quite easy to get part-way through an alteration and get distracted, so work right through the alteration, including the truing of the pattern, before you move on to the next alteration.

Sometimes you finish up removing some of the extra paper you have added on for one alteration when you get to the next one. This is fine: if you hadn't put it on with the first alteration you would probably be cutting the panel too small with the second one.

I like to take the pins out of the toile as I complete each of the alterations; this makes sure I do all the alterations I've pinned out during the fitting.

Bustline/Waistline in the Wrong Place

Time and time again I have seen ladies who think that if you redraw the line further up or down the pattern this is the alteration completed.

This is not the case. If you just redraw the line, it doesn't alter where the shaping is, so it makes no difference to the fit of the pattern.

When you do this alteration, you are moving the shaping on the pattern to be in the same place as the shaping is on your body.

The following pictures and steps show you how to do the alteration for *lowering* the bustline position.

If you are doing an alteration for *raising* the bustline you need to do the alteration in reverse by overlapping and folding. Similar alterations are sometimes needed on the waistline or hipline. If you need alterations on both your waistline and bustline, for example, you will be doing two separate alterations.

You will need to do this alteration on all the body pieces of the pattern if the

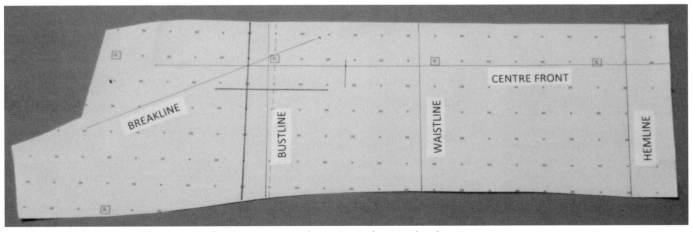

Bustline in wrong place, step 1, drawing the alteration.

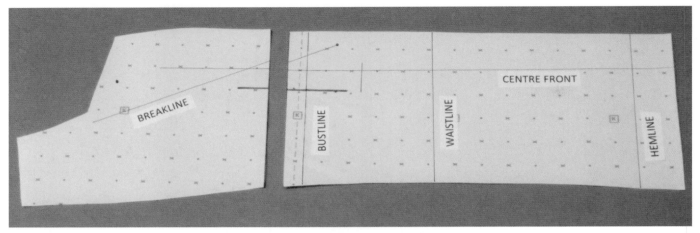

Bustline in wrong place, step 2, cutting through the pattern.

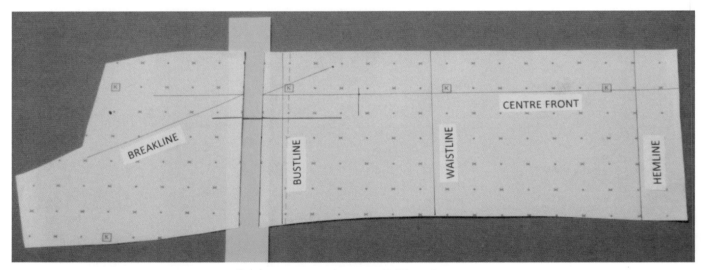

Bustline in wrong place, step 3, filling the gap.

alteration is equal all round.

Sometimes you only need to move the lines on either the front or the back, in which case you even the alteration out over the side body pieces.

1. Drawing the alteration on the pattern

Draw a line just above the bustline. It's easier to see where you are with the alteration if you don't cut through exactly on the bustline.

Draw another line at 90 degrees to the line above the bustline. This line is a balance line so you can match up the pattern once you cut through and open/close the pattern.

Drawing these lines in makes it easier to match up the pattern later.

2. Cutting through the pattern

Cut through the pattern on the line just above the bustline, then move the cut pieces open by the amount required for your alteration.

If you look at the pattern as you move it, you will see the bustline move down.

3. Filling the gap

Place a piece of pattern paper behind the opening. I'm using coloured paper on the photographs to make it easier for you to see; I usually use the same dot-and-cross paper.

Secure the new piece in place using Sellotape or similar adhesive tape.

That is the alteration completed in terms of moving the bustline down into the correct position for you, but you will have made the jacket longer by the

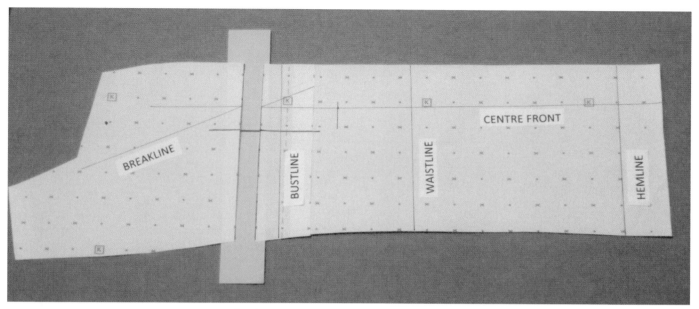

Bustline in wrong place, step 4, compensating.

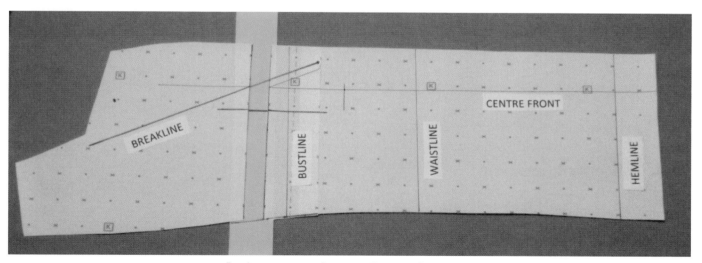

Bustline in wrong place, step 5, truing the pattern.

amount of the alteration.

This is where most people then get confused with alterations. The vast majority of people can identify the problem on the toile, they can also mark it onto the pattern and execute the alteration but then the pattern becomes distorted from the original; in this case it's fairly easy to see what has altered and get it back to shape, but in some cases it's not quite so obvious.

This is where compensation or truing of the pattern comes into play. It more often than not takes longer to do the truing than it does to do the alteration.

4. Compensating for the alteration
Mark in a line just below the bustline, then cut through it. Overlap the pattern by the same amount by which you opened out the pattern above the bustline.

5. Truing the pattern
Now look at the sides of the pattern and the break line. Both are distorted. True the sides of the pattern as described at the end of the chapter, by smoothing out the little steps at the sides of the pattern.

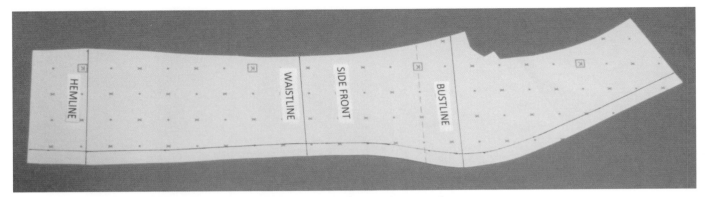

Bust increase, step 1, marking in the seam allowance.

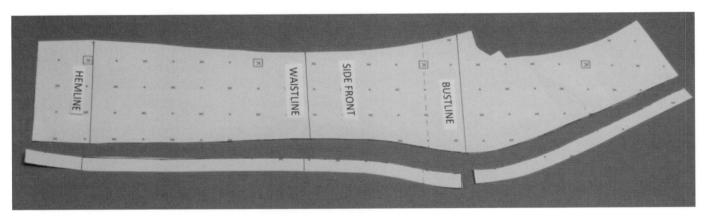

Bust increase, step 2, trimming the seam allowance.

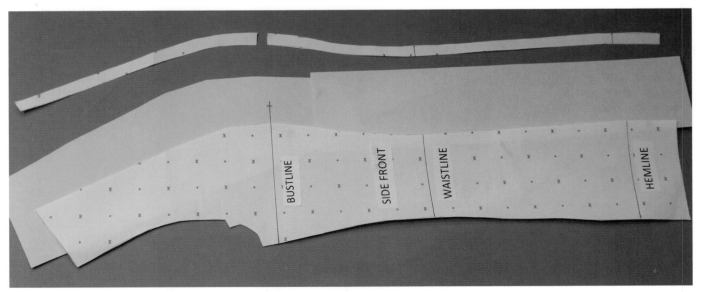

Bust increase, step 3, measuring the alteration.

Draw in a new line between the marks at each end of the break line; this becomes your new break line.

Bust Increase for Larger Cup Size

I have seen many overly complicated explanations of how to do this alteration. I think the following is a pretty straightforward way of doing it.

Calculate how much extra fabric is required in total.

Then divide this measurement by two; this is the amount needed to do the alteration. (Don't forget you are only working with half the pattern.)

1. Marking in the seam allowance

Mark in the seam allowance along the princess-line seam of the side front panel.

Make sure you have the bustline clearly marked in.

2. Trimming off the seam allowance

Trim off the seam allowance (but don't throw it away).

You are going to use this seam allowance as a guide for the alteration. Snip the seam allowance in two at the bustline.

3. Measuring the alteration

Put a new piece of paper underneath the pattern. Measure from the side body at the bustline by the amount of the alteration. Mark clearly where you are going to alter to.

4. Repositioning the seam allowance

Now reposition the two pieces of the seam allowance.

The ends of the seam allowance at the armhole edge and bottom of the panel should be back in their starting positions.

The cut edge should be repositioned by the amount required for the alteration, creating a gap between the original bustline and the cut edges of the seam allowance.

The cut through the bustline on the seam allowance will no longer meet, creating a gap at the bustline.

By using the original seam allowance of the pattern, you are able to keep the pattern extremely near to the original, and the new shape is very easy to draw without having lumps and bumps in the wrong place.

5. Redrawing the panel

Redraw the panel around the outside edge of the seam allowance. There will be a gap where you have cut through the seam allowance at the bustline. Measure this gap.

The front panel of the jacket will need to be altered as well. The amount by which you opened the bustline on the side front panel will need to be put into the centre front panel.

If you don't add this extra to the centre front panel, you won't be able to stitch the two panels together as the centre front panel will be shorter than the side front panel.

The extra length in the seam was created when you extended the pattern to create extra fabric for the bust.

6. Altering the centre front panel

Cut the centre front panel at the bustline and open out by the same amount as the gap in the side body panel.

Position a piece of paper to fill the gap. Trim off the edges of this piece of paper to match the original pattern.

That is all there is to this alteration, but I like to check my pattern pieces before I move on.

To do this, first of all lay the side body panel on top of the centre front panel, as if you were about to stitch the two pieces together.

Check along the seam allowance to make sure the panels will still match up. Make sure you are matching this seam along the 1.5cm (⅝in) seamline.

If you try to match the edges of the pattern it definitely won't fit back together successfully. If it doesn't match, true the pattern back to shape.

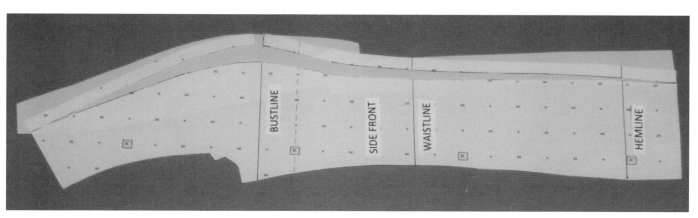

Bust increase, step 4, repositioning the seam allowance.

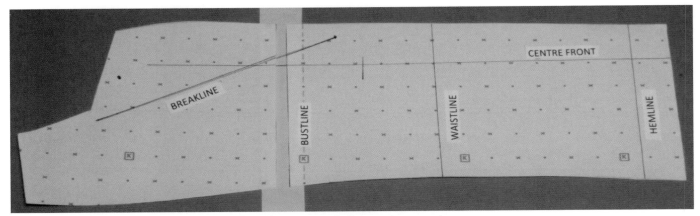

Bust increase, step 6, altering the centre front.

Shoulder Seam in the Wrong Place

If the shoulder seam is in the wrong place for your body shape, it can result in the jacket slipping back whilst you are wearing it. Most commonly this is cured by moving this seam forward.

Sometimes you don't have to move this line by the same amount right across the shoulder seam.

It could be that the seam is in the correct position at the neck edge and just out at the shoulder.

The alteration is simple.

1. Measuring the alteration

Measure how much you need to move the shoulder seam to get it into the correct position.

My photographs show the alteration for moving the seam forward evenly across the entire width of the shoulder.

2. Marking the pattern

Take the centre front and side front panels. Measuring down from the shoulder, mark in a line for the amount by which you need to move the seam forward.

If you are moving the seam by different amounts at each end of the

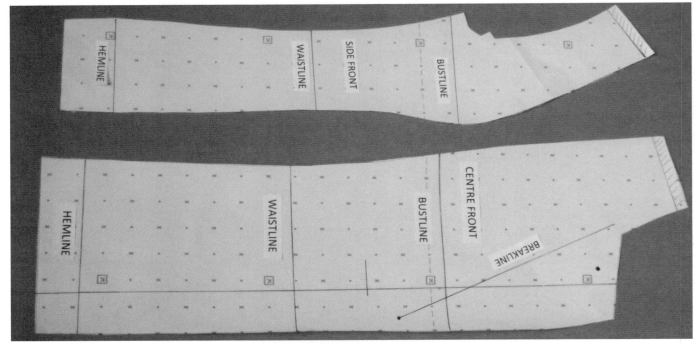

Shoulder alteration, step 2, marking the pattern.

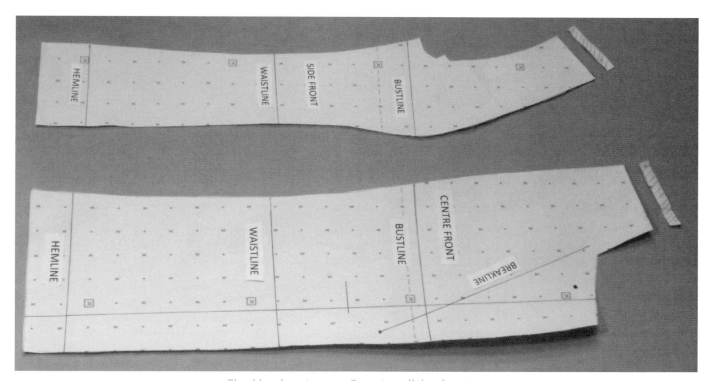

Shoulder alteration, step 3, cutting off the alteration.

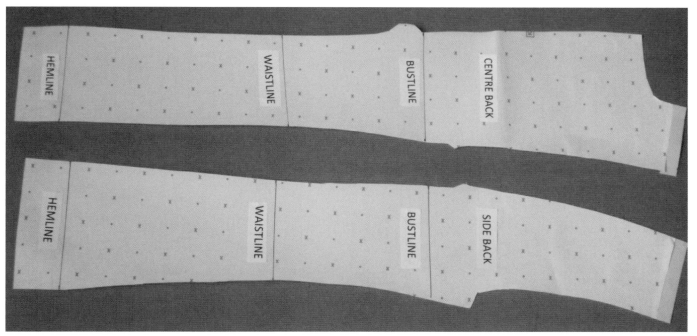

Shoulder alteration, step 4, adding to the back panels.

shoulder seam, make sure that you are taking off equal amounts on both sides of the princess-line seam, which falls in the middle of the shoulder.

3. Cutting off the alteration
Trim the pattern off along this line. You can throw away the pieces removed.

4. Adding to the back panels
Take the back panels and add a piece of paper to the shoulder seam measuring the same amount you have just cut off the front panels.

Don't use the piece you have just cut off the front panel as it most likely will not fit. It is also very fiddly to use a small piece of paper cut to a triangular shape.

Most of my students think that it's going to be easier to use the piece that has just been cut off the front panels, but the angles of the shoulders on the front and on the back of the pattern are different, so it is easier to redraw the shoulder seam, adding a new piece of paper to the pattern.

5. Truing the pattern back to shape
Check the shoulder seams to make sure they still fit together properly by laying the pattern pieces from the front of the jacket on top of the pieces for the back shoulder seam.

Lengthening or Shortening the Jacket Sleeves

When you pin this alteration whilst fitting the toile you will have to pin the length up from the bottom to shorten the sleeve or measure how much you need to add to make it the correct length. However, when you come to do the alteration, if you just cut the length off the bottom of the sleeve or add a piece to the bottom of the sleeve you will ruin the shape of the sleeve, especially if there is a vent opening, as on the pattern I'm using.

You will notice that both the upper and lower sleeve are quite shaped.

The photographs show the *shortening* of a sleeve. Have a look at the pattern pieces for the sleeves. You will probably see a lengthening and a shortening line; sometimes there may even be two, one just above the vent and one further up. If the amount you need to alter the pattern by is 3.1cm (1¼in) or less, you can use just one of the marked lines.

If it's more than that, you need to divide the amount by two and use both lengthening/shortening lines or make an extra cut through the pattern a bit further up both pattern pieces.

By splitting the alteration to two places, it limits the disruption to the shape of the sleeve.

This makes it easier to maintain the shape of the sleeve, keeping it as near to the original pattern as possible.

1. Marking the pattern for alteration
Using the lengthening/shortening line on the pattern as a starting point, measure and mark a second line on the pattern to indicate the amount by which you want to shorten the sleeve. The pieces of the pattern will be overlapped once the pattern is cut through.

If you are *lengthening* the sleeve you will need to cut through the pattern and open it out by the required amount.

Make sure you also mark in the

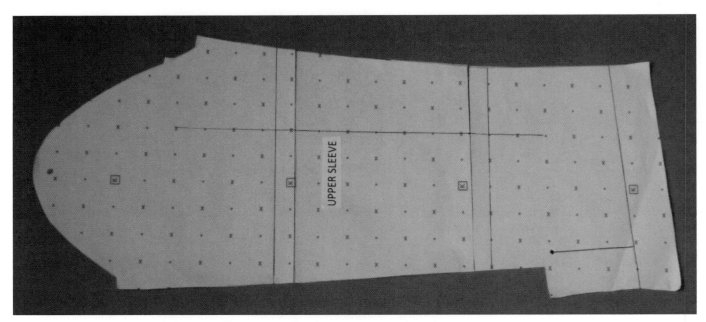

Shortening jacket sleeves, step 1, marking the pattern.

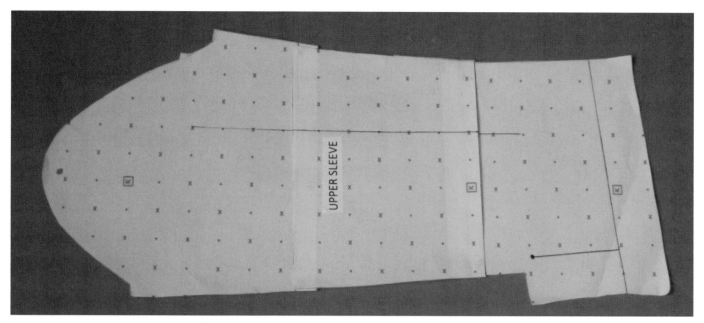

Shortening jacket sleeves, step 2, cutting through the pattern.

straight grain line so the pattern can be lined up correctly when the alteration is done.

2. Cutting through the pattern
Cut through the line. I find that cutting through the pattern makes it easier to do an accurate alteration, rather than just folding it over.

Either open (to lengthen it) or overlap it (to shorten it). If you need to do two cuts for your alteration, repeat this step at the higher mark.

When you put the pattern back together, line up the straight grain line; this keeps the pattern on the original straight grain, so when you lay the pattern out on your fabric it will lie exactly as the pattern was drafted to do.

You will need to repeat this alteration for the lower sleeve as well as the upper sleeve, as shown in the pictures.

3. Truing the pattern back to shape
You will notice that the sides of the pattern pieces look as if they have small steps along the seams.

This is where you need to true the

pattern back to shape.

Taking in Seams

This is probably the easiest of the alterations to do, but you will need to take extra care when truing the pattern back to shape. You need both of the pattern pieces for the panels where you are taking in the seam.

The photographs show the process of taking in the princess-line seam at the back of the jacket.

1. Marking the position for the alteration on the pattern
Measure to the first pin on the seamline. (It doesn't matter whether you start at the top or the bottom of the seam.)

Remember the toile has the hem at the bottom and the seam at the top folded inside, so add these seam allowances to your measurement when marking pattern.

Measure to the same distance from the top or bottom of the pattern. Put a dot on

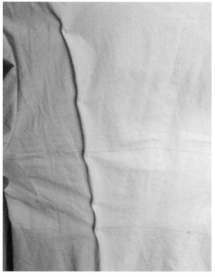

Taking in seams.

the paper. This is where the alteration will start.

2. Measuring how much to take in
Measure from the edge of the alteration to the pin. Mark in by the same distance from the edge of the pattern.

Continue along the seam, marking

Taking in seams, step 1, marking the alteration.

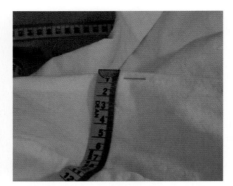

Taking in seams, step 2, measuring the alteration.

each pin position on the pattern with a series of dots. Remember you will need to mark all these positions on both of the panel pieces making up the seam.

Don't try to mark in one side of the seam, cut it off and then try to draw it on the other side using the bit cut off from the first side. The panels are different shapes, creating the shaping for the

jacket; if they were the same you wouldn't get the shaping you need for a human body.

3. Joining up the dots
Using a ruler, join all the dots on your pattern in a nice gentle curving line, as near to the original shape of the pattern as possible, whilst taking in the amount needed.

If the alteration does not go right to the top and/or bottom of the pattern piece, you will need to graduate the line you are drawing out to the side of the pattern.

Make this line as smooth as you can; you will be extending the alteration beyond the first and last pin on your toile, but that's fine.

I can guarantee that you don't go in sharply at any point on your body.

Trim the pattern off along the line you have just drawn.

4. Checking the pattern
Before you move on, lay the two pieces of pattern together one on top of the other, as if you were about to sew them together.

If you are taking in the princess-line seams, either back or front, lay the side body panel on top of the centre panel. In both cases you are checking to see if they still fit together neatly along the seamline, *not* the edge.

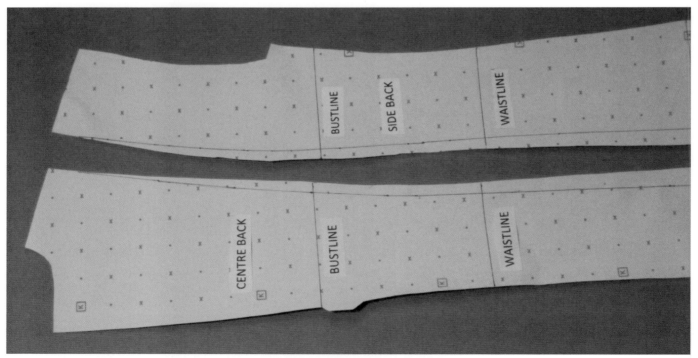

Taking in seams, step 3, joining the dots.

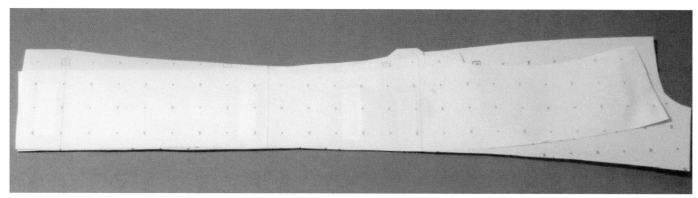

Taking in seams, step 4, checking the pattern.

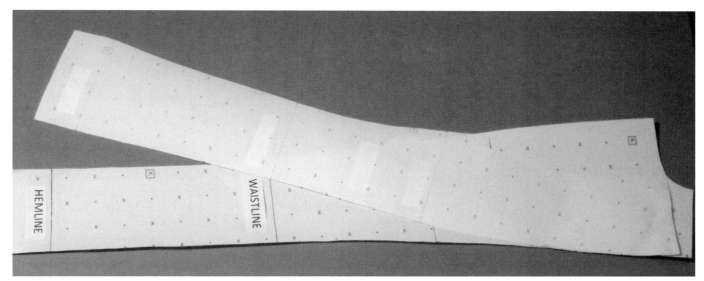

HEMLINE

WAISTLINE

Taking in seams, one longer than the other.

Chances are that one will be longer than the other.

Put a pin into the pattern exactly where the seamline will be. Then open out the two pattern pieces as if you had just stitched them together.

This will reveal the amount of the step you need to true up.

5. Truing the pattern
True the pattern by smoothing out the step you have just measured. Add a bit to one side and take a bit from the other.

Look for full details under 'Truing the pattern' later in this chapter.

Allowing for a Sway Back

If you need this alteration there will be an excess of fabric folding horizontally either above or around the waistline at the back of the jacket.

The same amount may not need to be removed across the whole back, and the fold may extend as far as the side front panel. Pin out the amount required when doing the fitting for the jacket.

If you think about the alteration in its entirety it will look like an exceptionally long thin dart running horizontally around the jacket.

1. Measuring the position for the alteration
Measure down to the alteration on the toile, then measure the same distance on the pattern.

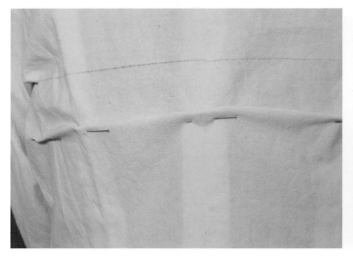

Pinning the alteration for a sway back.

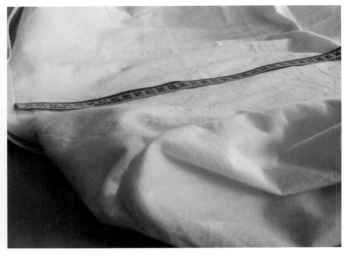

Sway back, step 1, measuring the position.

Sway back, step 2, measuring the size of alteration.

You will need to take a measurement at all the pin positions you have placed in the toile.

Draw a straight line joining up the marks you have just measured, going across the two (or more, depending on how far your alteration goes around the jacket) pattern pieces.

2. Measuring the size of the alteration
Measure from your pin to the edge of the fabric fold. Remember to double this amount, as there is the same measurement on both sides of the pin.

Measure at each pin; the size of the alteration will probably vary at each point.

3. Marking the alteration on the pattern
Mark this measurement below the first one. Take several measurements as you go across the back panels.

Sway back, step 3, marking the alteration.

When you get to the seams make sure you remove the same amount from both sides of the seam when you go on to the next panel.

When you get to the end of the alteration it will go out to nothing, just like the end of a dart.

Don't make the end of the alteration finish abruptly; it is better to extend it slightly than trying to have a steep difference in the alteration.

4. Cutting through the pattern

When you have marked out on the pattern the full amount to be removed, cut through the first line you drew and overlap the panel to the second line.

Secure the piece back together using adhesive tape.

Don't worry if the panels look a bit skew-whiff; they will do if you have taken unequal amounts from either side of the panel.

5. Truing up the straight grain lines

Place a ruler on the two ends of the original straight grain line and draw a straight line. (See 'Truing the pattern' for

picture.)

This will be your new straight grain when measuring the placement of your pattern on the fabric..

Place each of the panels on top of the panel it joins to and check the length of each seam. True the pattern where necessary.

Truing the Pattern

On all the photographs for this section I have exaggerated the alteration so that it is more visible. In some cases I have substituted a square of pattern paper instead of the original pattern to make it clearer.

Sometimes the alteration on the pattern is exceedingly small, but it is worth doing this truing to keep the pattern as near to the original as possible.

Side of the pattern not running smoothly

1. Assessing the alteration

Look on the side of the pattern once the alteration is complete and you will find that the edges of the pattern are not running in a smooth line. There will be at least one little step, if not a series, along the side of the pattern.

2. Marking up the alteration

Measure each step and then divide the measurement in half. Mark this second measurement onto the step in the pattern.

Then draw a new line from just above the step to just below it, going through the mark on the step.

This line will true the pattern back to shape: you are taking a small piece from one side of the step and adding a small piece to the other side, thus balancing it up.

Don't forget you are trying to keep the pattern as near as possible to the original so follow the same basic shape as the edge of the original pattern piece.

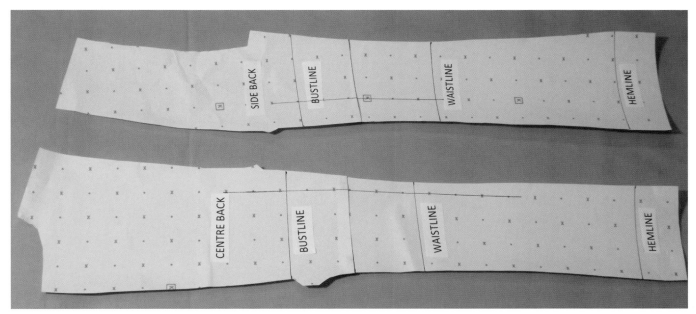

Sway back, step 4, cutting the pattern.

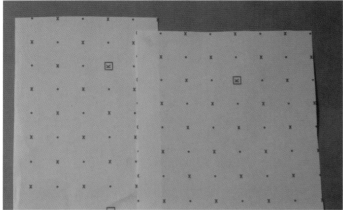

Truing the pattern, step 1, assessing the alteration.

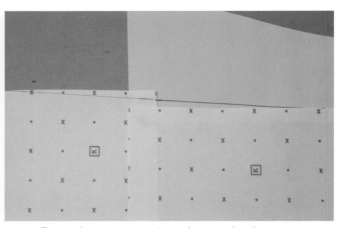

Truing the pattern step 2, marking up the alteration.

I find that most students try to make this smoothing out of the pattern too abrupt and finish up with corners on the pattern. Smooth it out gradually; a longer smoother line is better than a short abrupt one.

Seam length not matching

You need to measure to see if this correction is needed for the seams on all the panels you have altered.

The differences created when you take in a seam, due to the shape of the panels, may give you a step at the top or bottom of the pattern piece. To true this alteration to shape you will need to measure the seams.

1. Measuring the size of the alteration

Lay the two pieces of pattern for the seam together, one on top of the other, as if you were going to pin the seam to sew it. If you are measuring the princess-line seam, it is easier to have the side body on top.

Work the pieces together considering all the shaping. When you are measuring the seam, you aren't measuring along the edge of the pattern, you are measuring along the seamline. When I'm measuring, I run my finger along the seamline instead of pinning it all the way along.

2. Stabilizing the seamline

When you get to the top of the seam, you will probably find that one piece is longer than the other.

Put a pin into the seamline at the top and open the two pieces of pattern out flat. This will give you a better idea of where you are going to alter the pieces.

You should see a step at the top of the pattern.

In the photograph I've shown the shoulder for the alteration, but the alteration could occur in the armhole, depending on where the seam shaping ends.

Truing seam length, step 1, measuring the alteration.

3. Reshaping the pattern

Stick a piece of paper under the short side of the alteration. Make sure it extends into the seam allowance you have pinned through.

As with the edges of pattern piece trued up earlier, you need to measure the step and divide it in half. Mark this measurement on the pattern and then redraw the pattern, keeping the shape as near to the original pattern as possible. You will be adding a small amount to one side of the step and taking a small amount off the other side.

Trim along the marked line. When you unpin the seam, you will find that your alteration is complete, including the correction where the seam allowance is.

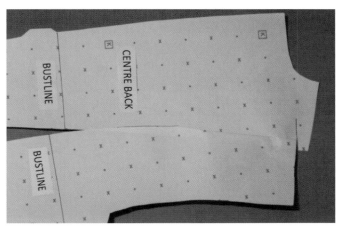

Truing seam length, step 2, stabilizing the seamline.

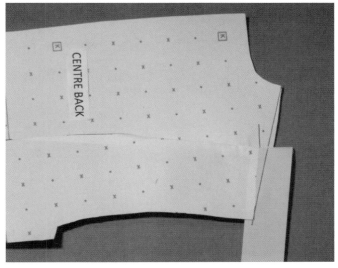

Truing seam length, step 3, reshaping the pattern.

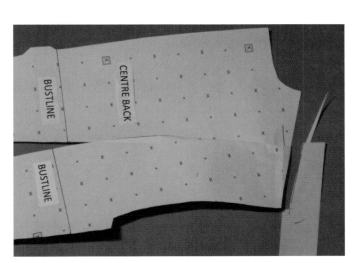

Truing the seam length, step 4, final trim.

Taking out the bumps and hollows

If you make an alteration on the pattern, where you take out more on one side of the pattern than the other (for example, the sway back alteration), you will need to straighten out both the sides and the straight grain lines.

1. Straightening the grain line
Once the pattern piece is stuck back together with adhesive tape, look at the straight grain line. It will look very bowed in the middle.

To straighten it up, place your ruler so that it connects one end of the original straight grain line to the other, then draw a new straight line (shown in red here).

2. Reviewing the sides
Look at the side of the pattern; it will appear very bowed outwards on one side and an inward V shape will have appeared on the other.

3. Straightening out the sides
Start with the inward V shape and draw a curved line smoothing it out so that it looks more like the original pattern. (I have used a straight line here only for emphasis.)

Measure how much extra you have added to the pattern piece to smooth it out.

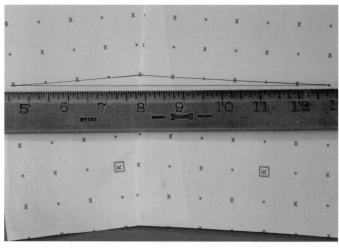

Bumps and hollows, step 1, straightening the grain line.

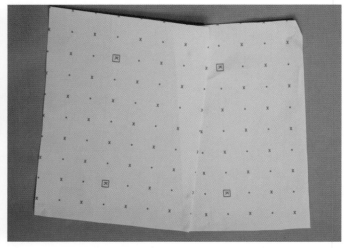

Bumps and hollows, step 2, reviewing the sides.

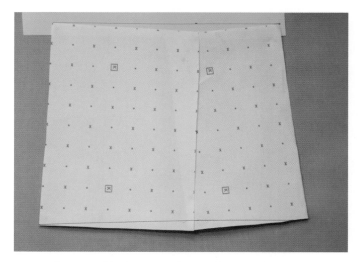

Bumps and hollows, step 3, straightening the sides.

Take away the same amount from the outward bowed side of the pattern and trim off.

This will have brought your pattern back to as near to the original pattern as you can whilst taking in the amount of alteration you require.

If you have a lot of alterations to do, it might be worthwhile making another toile to get a perfect fit.

I like to redraft the pattern at this stage too: it's much easier to work with a clean pattern.

When you redraft the pattern, make sure that you have all the pattern pieces on the straight grain.

If you use dot-and-cross paper, all the dots and crosses are straight grain lines, and you could use any of them when measuring from the edge of the cloth.

You can, of course, draw a line along any of the dots and crosses if you want to stick to the way the patterns do the job; then you can work from just the one line.

I've marked this on the pattern pieces I'm using, so it makes it clear to you in the photographs.

Once you have the pattern correctly fitting, you will never need to do another pattern, just alter this one for style, *providing* you maintain the same weight as you are when you do the fitting.

Chapter 4

Cutting Out

Now you have completed the fitting of the jacket using the toile you can go ahead and cut the jacket out. I'm going to use the dressmaker's way of doing it as it keeps all the seam allowances the same size and it is less confusing if this is the first jacket you have made.

If the fitting and alterations stage has been done properly you shouldn't need any extra in the seams as the traditional tailors do.

Before you start to cut you will need to pre-shrink your fabric. Not all fabric will shrink, but it's better not to chance it. You will be doing quite a lot of pressing whilst you make up the jacket and the pieces of the jacket may well shrink during this process if you don't do it first.

Lay the fabric on your ironing board folded in half, right side out and selvedges together. Hover your steam iron over the fabric about 3mm (⅛in) above the surface of the fabric.

You don't need to touch the fabric but you do need to get close enough for the steam to get into the fabric.

Go to about 5cm (2in) from the fold. As you work your way along the length of the fabric fold it over onto a table. Don't let the fabric dangle over the edge of the ironing board as you will stretch out the fabric you have just shrunk. Steam over one side of the fabric and then turn it over and do the other side.

Once both sides have been done, open out the fold and steam up the middle of the fabric.

Whilst you are doing this job look out for any flaws in the fabric. Mark them with a pin going through both sides of the fabric. The fault may not go all the way across the width of the fabric and if you lay the fabric upside down to the fault when you are cutting out, you may not see it. With a pin in it you can easily see where the faults are.

Check the fold of the fabric for dirty or faded areas. This is a common fault with fabric, and you don't want it in the middle of your jacket.

When you have steamed all over the fabric, you must leave it to one side, folded up, until all the steam has dried out before you start cutting out.

Identifying the Right Side of Your Fabric

The selvedge is usually the first place to look to decide on the right side of the fabric. Traditional tailoring cloth usually has the maker's name and/or what the fabric is made from along the selvedge. This is woven so that the writing is visible from the right side of the cloth.

The other clue that the selvedge can give you is the series of holes on the edge; they tend to be raised on the wrong side. Another clue is the weave of the cloth: if the diagonal weave runs from bottom left to top right of a square, this is the right side.

The feel of the nap on the cloth can also give away the right side. Run your hands both ways along the length of the cloth to see which feels best. Generally the cloth should smooth downwards, but in some cases the fabric looks better if it smooths up.

The colour of a napped fabric can be different in both directions as well.

If your fabric has a nap on it, you will need to make sure that all your pattern pieces are lying in the same direction.

You won't be able to turn the panels round to make them fit more easily on the fabric.

In some cases, you may need to buy extra cloth if the fabric has a nap.

Sometimes you just have to admit that the right side of the cloth is not obvious. In this case, I decide which side I like the best and, when I've cut out the

Shrinking the fabric.

SUPER 120ˢ WOOL AND PURE CASHMERE

Selvedge edge.

Straightening the edge of the cloth.

pieces, I use tailor's chalk to mark a cross on each piece on the wrong side. Chalking the wrong side makes it quick and easy when you are making up the jacket.

When laying out the cloth ready for cutting out, I fold the fabric so that the right side is on the inside. I do it this way because it makes it easier to spot the right side after you have done the tailor tacks once the cutting out is done.

Straightening the Edge of the Cloth

Before you start to lay your pattern pieces out on the cloth, check the ends of the fabric. Sometimes the edge isn't cut very straight and one edge doesn't extend as far as the other; in the tailoring trade this is known as a bum lay.

You can either straighten up the edge of the cloth by fraying it out, or mark a chalk line on to the edge so that you know where the cloth is level.

Cutting the Main Fabric

Laying out the pieces

I start with the jacket body panels first. These are the biggest pieces so they need to be placed onto the fabric first; the smaller pieces can be placed around them and are much easier to fit onto the fabric afterwards.

1. Centre back
I start with the centre back, laying this next to the folded edge. If your pattern has no seam on the centre back panel, place the centre back onto the fold of the fabric.

Be careful that you don't get a gap between the fold of the fabric and the edge of the pattern; if this happens you will make the back panel larger.

2. Side back
Now lay the side body next to it. These pieces will, of course, eventually be stitched together; although they are not exactly the same shape, you will be able to fit them quite closely together.

3. Side front
You will get a third panel piece next to that (usually the side front).

These three pieces will probably take up the entire width of the fabric, although the pattern and size that I'm using allows me to place a fourth pattern piece across the width.

4. Front facing
The front facing should fit alongside the body panels.

In my layout, I managed to get this piece in between the panels on the first width of the layout.

On the front facing, cut as per the pattern on the edge where it will join the lining.

On its front edge, you don't need to cut the shape of the pattern; I just cut out an oblong in the fabric. Use tailor's chalk to mark this extra fabric whilst you are laying out the pattern: you won't remember to cut the extra if you don't.

By allowing extra on this front edge it gives you a bit of what I like to call wiggle room when basting under the jacket.

5. Centre front
Now move along the fabric from the first row of body panel pattern pieces, laying the centre front panel and any other body panels side by side.

6. Sleeves
Depending on the size and the pattern you are using, you may be able to lay one piece of the sleeve alongside the body panels.

The other sleeve piece will be placed above the first one.

As you can see from my photographs, I have placed the upper sleeve between the side body panel and the centre front panel.

7. Collar
The two pieces for the collar will fit on

Laying out pattern pieces.

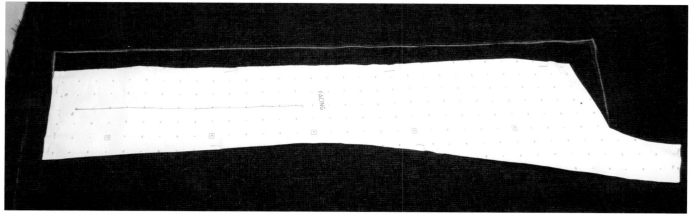

Front facing.

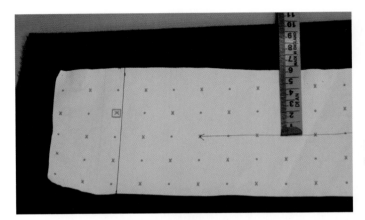

Measuring straight grain line.

the fabric left at the end of the piece.

The under collar is on the cross grain or bias. This will allow for the under collar to be shaped around the neck edge later on. If your pattern doesn't have the under collar on the cross grain, you can easily change the grain line.

First, draw a line at 90 degrees to the fold on the pattern. Then draw a line which bisects the square you have made at the centre back; this line will be at 45

Centre front and sleeves.

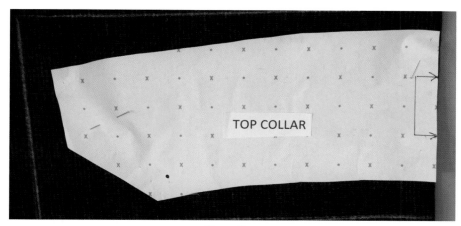

Top collar.

Cutting out.

degrees to the centre back; in other words, it has a cross grain line. You will also have to add a 1.5cm (⅝in) seam to the centre back seam.

The top collar is on the fold of the fabric.

When I'm cutting the top collar, I just cut an oblong of fabric bigger than the pattern.

Again, mark the extra with tailor's chalk; this will allow for adjustments when hand-stitching the collar later.

Note: Now check again that everything is on the correct grain and that you have all the pieces you need for your jacket. Don't miss this stage out. It seems like a bit of a pain checking everything again

TIPS FOR CUTTING OUT

When you cut out make sure you use the full length of the shears to make a cut. Lots of people like to nibble along the edge of the pattern using about 2.5cm (1in) of the blade and then ask why they have jagged edges. If you use the full length of the blade and close the shears at the end of each stroke you will make a smoother cut. Closing the shears at the end of each cut will take the pressure off your thumb joint every time you cut. This means you won't get an ache in your thumb joint if you have a lot of cutting out to do. You need to cut as close to the edge of the pattern as you can, without cutting into it. Take your time and cut accurately. Don't rush and leave extra fabric around the edge of the pattern. You have taken lots of time making this pattern fit; don't spoil it by rushing the cutting-out process.

but it's worth doing just in case you have missed a piece of pattern.

At this stage you can rejig the layout to accommodate a missed piece, but this might not be possible if you have cut out the jacket before discovering the mistake.

Pinning the pattern pieces in place

In the tailoring workrooms pins are not used for cutting out. The pattern is laid on to the cloth and then held down by a tailor's weight. The pattern piece is carefully marked in, using white tailor's chalk all round the edge of the pattern.

The inlays (seams allowances) are then marked in. This can be very confusing if you haven't done it before, so I'm going to pin the pattern onto the fabric the way dressmakers are used to doing it.

As long as the pattern pieces are cut accurately it won't make any difference to the jacket.

Don't pin the pieces onto the fabric until you are sure of the position of the piece.

When pinning, pin the edge of the pattern within the seam allowance. Some fabric can be damaged by the pins, but if you put the pins within the seam allowance you won't leave marks on the fabric where they might show.

Once I have measured the straight grain line, I put a weight in the middle of the panels. You don't need any fancy expensive weights; a couple of washed stones out of the garden will do the job, or a can of baked beans from the store cupboard. It's only a temporary measure until you can get the pins into the edges.

You don't need any army of pins either. I always put a pin at each corner of each piece and then one about every 20cm (8in). You need enough to stabilize the pattern whilst you cut out but not too many that they get in your way. Make

sure the pattern stays flat whilst you pin the whole of the piece.

Avoid any folds or creases in the pattern; this should be fairly easy to do with the dot-and-cross paper whereas the ordinary tissue paper on which a commercial pattern is usually drafted tends to crease more readily.

Check everything is perfect before you start to cut out. The saying 'Measure twice, cut once' applies to cutting out fabric as well as the original usage referring to woodwork.

Cutting out the pieces

Don't worry about cutting any more pieces beyond the major ones listed so far.

All the pocket pieces will come out of the spare fabric left when the bigger pieces have been cut. The details of the pieces you will need are in Chapter 5, but for the moment they don't need to be cut.

Some of the pieces are quite small and have a habit of getting lost or falling off the table, so just save all the pieces of spare fabric.

I like to wrap all the spare fabric

pieces together and tie a spare length of fabric around them; this makes sure you don't lose anything.

If you need to mark the wrong side on any of these pieces, do it now with tailor's chalk.

Tailor Tacks

Before you take any pins out of the pattern pieces you will need to mark the pieces using tailor tacks (also known as mark stitches or stitch marks). There are lots of very long-winded ways of doing these tacks but it is a lot quicker if you use basting thread (*see* Chapter 1 for the description of this thread).

The following positions need to be marked:

- Centre front panel: hemline, centre front, break line, top button, magic dot (see the section 'Making the Toile' for details of this dot), pocket position
- Side front panel: hemline
- Side body panel: hemline, dot at the side seam position
- Side back panel: hemline
- Centre back panel: hemline
- Upper sleeve: dot at the head of the

Tailor tacks, running stitch.

Marking a line of tailor tacks.

sleeve, hemline, vent fold line
- Lower sleeve: hemline, dot at the underarm for the side seam placement
- Under collar: magic dot.

Making the tailor tacks

1. Running stitch
To make this process quick and easy, use a double thread and make a running stitch where you need the mark to be.

If it's just a single mark, such as the one where the shoulder position is on the upper sleeve, pull the thread through to leave a 1.5cm (⅝in) tail. Then simply trim off the thread leaving the same amount of tail on the other side of the stitch.

Note: Don't leave the ends of your tailor tacks too long, even if you think it will be easier to pull them out if they are longer: they will get caught up in everything.

2. Removing the pattern
Whether the tacks are single, multiple or in corners, removing the pattern is done in the same way.

On each piece, check all the tacks have been sewn. Snip through any loops. Remove all the pins from the edges of the pattern, then carefully lift the pattern off the cut piece. Make sure you don't pull out any of the tailor tacks as you do this.

3. Separating the pieces
Ease the two layers of fabric apart until you have enough of the tailor tack stitch to enable you to cut through the middle, then trim through the threads.

You now have a tack on each panel in matched places.

4. Marking a line of tailor tacks
If you are marking a line of stitches you place the first stitch as before but then do all the others in the line before pulling the thread through to the first stitch leaving a tail about 1.5cm (⅝in) long; trim the other side of the stitch to about 1.5cm (⅝in). This is your first tailor tack in place. Now pull the thread via the needle to the same distance from your second tailor tack. Leave the tail as before and trim, just the same as the first tailor tack, and continue until you get to the last of your stitches.

You don't need an army of tailor tacks; one about every 7.5cm (3in) is sufficient unless it is a small piece you are marking or a more complicated panel (for instance, one which has a dart or pleat). The stitches will stay in place until you are ready to remove them once they are no longer needed, as you progress through making up the jacket. If you put too many stitches in, it takes ages to remove them and they can get trapped in the seams if you are not careful.

Tailor tacking a corner
If you are marking a corner with tailor tacks, make sure that you have one side of the tailor tack going into the corner from both directions. By marking it in

Tailor tacks, separating the pieces.

this way, you will have two halves of the tailor tack in the corner and you will be able to easily read their positions.

Fold the remaining fabric and put it to one side along with the collar pieces. Smooth out the pattern pieces and put them to one side ready for cutting out the lining but pick out the centre front panel pattern, which is needed for the next stage.

Tailor tacks, removing the pattern.

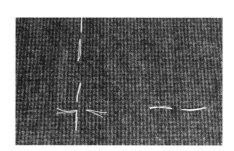

Tailor tacking a corner.

Cutting the Lining

When you cut out the lining pieces, some adjustments have to be made to the pattern so that the lining fits the jacket. Most of these adjustments just involve leaving some extra fabric in certain places around the pattern piece.

You may end up cutting off these extra pieces as you make up the rest of the jacket, but you need to create this safety net just in case. Fabric can move around and, in some cases, distort when you are making up the jacket. By allowing this extra fabric, you don't have to worry about anything going wrong.

The centre front panel is the exception as you need to cut an extra piece of pattern to accommodate the front facing.

On the rest of the pattern I just draw in the extra amounts needed on the lining before I cut out; there is no need to draft out another pattern.

If you just follow the rules for each panel as listed below you can't go wrong. The lining will be a perfect fit every time.

Cutting the centre front panel

You need to make the panel for the centre front first so that you can make allowances for it when you cut the lining out.

The centre front panel will be mostly covered by the front facing but if you lay the front facing over the centre front panel you will find that it doesn't cover the whole piece.

This is because the jacket would become very bulky if you cut the whole of the front in another layer of your main fabric.

A new pattern piece is needed to cover this section; to make this piece proceed as follows.

1. Laying the facing onto the pattern

Lay the front facing over the centre front panel, making sure the pieces are matching at the top, the bottom and the front edge.

You may find that the facing pattern piece is slightly bigger than the centre front around the lapel area.

Just let it sit over the edge. Don't worry; it will only be a slight amount that the pattern company has allowed for the 'roll' of the cloth.

This will be explained in more detail in Chapter 7; it is just another tailoring term designed to make it sound more complicated than it really is. You won't even know you have done it. And you certainly don't need a maths degree to work it out.

2. Marking the edge of the facing

Using a pen or pencil, mark the inside edge of the facing onto the centre front panel.

3. Marking in the seam allowance

Remove the facing pattern from the centre front.

Draw a second line parallel to the one you have just marked, closer to the front edge by 3.1cm (1¼in).

This distance is the width of two seam allowances.

Make sure you transfer the straight grain line onto the pattern piece; use the centre front panel as a guide to get this right.

4. Tracing off the new pattern

Trace off the pattern along the new seamline and include all the side and armhole edges from the front pattern.

The new pattern piece will be cut in lining.

When you join up the lining, this piece will be joined to the facing. The new pattern and the facing panel piece will then cover the entire centre front panel of the jacket.

You are now ready to cut out the lining.

I love patterned linings as well as the beautiful satin linings, which are a little bit heavier than normal dress linings.

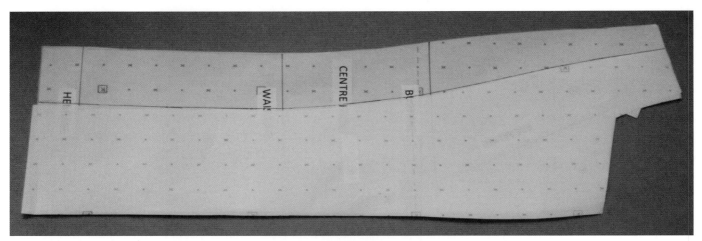

Laying front facing onto the pattern.

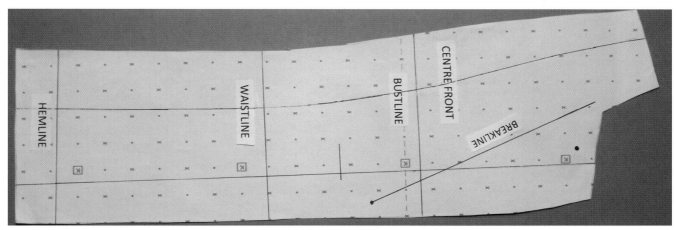

Marking the edge of the facing.

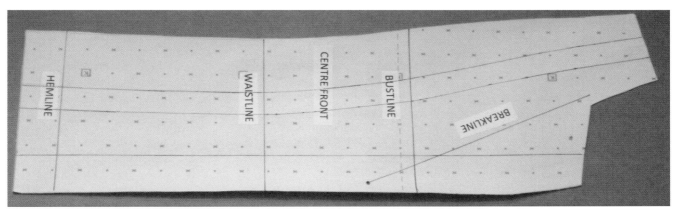

Marking in the seam allowance.

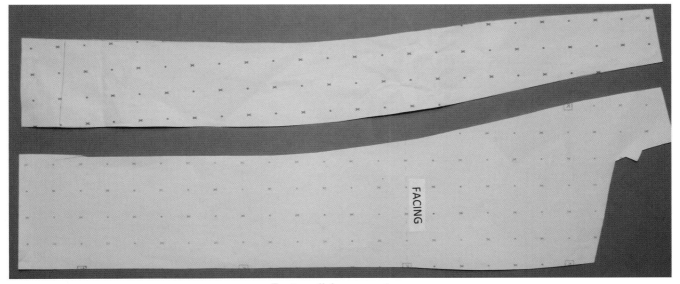

Tracing off the new pattern.

I like to cut all my lining pieces from the same lining, although tailoring workrooms use a different lining for the sleeves of a gentleman's jacket. The sleeve lining is a heavier lining, usually cream with pinstripes of different colours in it: this extra thickness makes the sleeve lining harder wearing. This is because men tend to wear a jacket every day and take it off and put it on more frequently than women, so the sleeve lining is under more pressure than the body lining.

Cutting the other body lining panels

1. Centre back panel

Place this panel on the fold in the lining, even if your pattern has a seam in the main fabric. This is because a 5cm (2in) pleat is needed in the centre back lining rather than a seam. This pleat allows you to reach forward with your arms when wearing the jacket without splitting the lining.

The pattern I'm using already has a 1.5cm (⅝in) seam included in the pattern, so I need to allow an extra 1cm (⅜in) to this edge.

This will give me 2.5cm (1in) measurement for the fold. When you measure the complete width of the pleat, both sides of the fold, this will give you the 5cm (2in) needed for the whole pleat.

Measure 1cm (⅜in) at the top and bottom of the centre back panel and then place the pattern on the marks. **Note:** The waistline of the pattern will be further in than the 1cm (⅜in) measured. This is not a problem; the extra will be taken in when you lay the lining in place.

If your pattern is cut to be on a fold, place the top and bottom of the pattern piece 2.5cm (1in) from the fold. **Note:** As a safety measure, mark a chalk line from the edge of the centre back to the fold at both top and bottom of the panel. This will stop you from cutting down the edge of the pattern, instead of leaving it against the fold.

You need to leave an extra 1.3cm (½in) on the armhole, neckline and shoulders of the centre back panel.

2. Other body panels

On all the other body pieces you will need to leave 1.3cm (½in) on the armhole edges, and the same amount on

the shoulder seam if your panel goes into this seam.

3. Sleeve panels

Eliminate the vent on the sleeve lining by trimming off the excess allowed at the bottom of the sleeves for the vent: you only need an ordinary 1.5cm (⅝in) seam allowance hre.

Just fold your pattern in along a line which is 1.5cm (⅝in) away from the fold line for the vent. This line should form a continuous smooth seamline from the top to the bottom of the sleeve.

You need extra in the sleeve seams to give some ease, so on both of the sleeve pattern pieces leave 3mm (⅛in) extra at the top of the seam.

At the elbow, cut the seam as the pattern.

At the bottom of the sleeve leave another 3mm (⅛in) extra.

This gives you some spare fabric when you make up the armholes; you are going to hand-finish the armholes of the jacket, so this extra is needed.

At the armhole edge of the sleeve pieces you will need to leave 1.3cm (½in) extra allowance.

Don't skip this section and hope that the lining will fit or use the lining

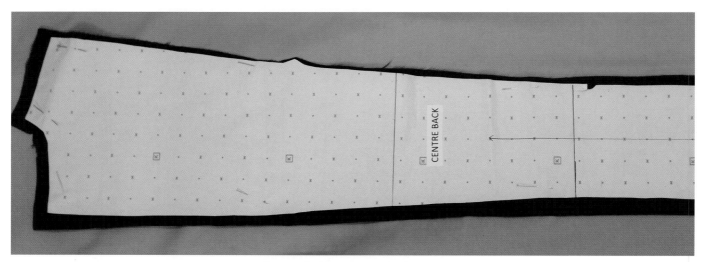

Cutting the lining centre back panel.

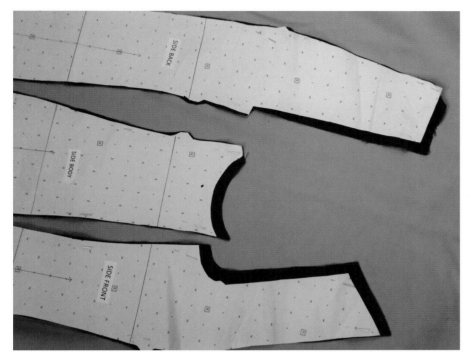

Body panels.

pattern provided by the pattern companies. They put lining into the jacket in a completely different way from the techniques I'm going to show you.

Fabric can distort whilst you are sewing and pressing it, so I prefer to have this safety net that I have outlined. It's better to trim off extra fabric than to have to join in a piece of lining or, worse, remake the whole of the jacket lining because you don't have enough fabric.

There are a few other pieces to be cut out of the lining and other fabrics but I will show you how to do them when I get to the relevant sections in the making-up process.

They are quite small pieces and would probably get lost before you need them.

At this stage I fold up all the pattern pieces. I like to get the pattern out of the way as soon as I can, as it clutters everywhere up and some of the pieces can go missing or get torn.

A lot of effort has been put into getting the pattern to fit, so you don't want any of the pieces going astray now.

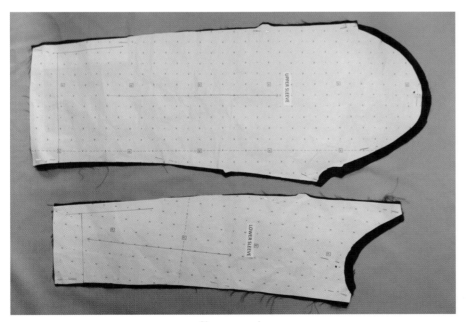

Sleeve panels.

Chapter 5

Joining the Pieces

Finally, after all that preparation you get to start sewing properly.

I like to do all the first-phase sewing and then press everything together. I am always being asked about which direction to stitch the seams. Years ago, it was always recommended to stitch everything from the top to the bottom. Sewing machines used to be quite basic and the dog feed didn't always work in the way it should; if you machined everything in one direction it meant that the fabric all dragged the same way, which more or less solved the problem of the panels looking distorted.

Today the technology of the machines is vastly improved so there is no need to do that.

The way I'm going to show you to stitch can't all be done in one direction.

Separate all the main jacket panel pieces from the lining pieces and put them in two separate piles; this means you can get on with the sewing-up without interruption.

Jacket Panels

Pinning and sewing your seams

When you pin two pieces of fabric together, make sure that you pin with the seamline to the right-hand side of your pin, point going towards the left. If you do this, you will never have the pins going in the wrong direction when you

Pinning the seams.

bring the fabric to the machine. (Left-handed readers may find it easier to turn the entire piece of work round to do this and then turn it back again to machine it.)

Remember that all these seams are 1.5cm (⅝in) wide. Try to be as accurate as you can when stitching them.

Start with the main jacket fabric and join the main body pieces first by stitching the princess-line seams between the centre front panel and the side front. This can be a quite a tricky seam to sew due to the different shapes of the two panels.

Pinning the flat part of the seam.

Here is a quick and easy way of doing it.

1. Pinning the flat part of the seam

Pin the seam from the bottom of the panels, with the side body panel on top. and parallel to the edge of the fabric. By pinning this way, you are creating a line of pins which form a mock stitching line. You will be securing about 1.3cm (½in) of fabric every time you pin, making the seam more secure when machining. You can pull the pins out of the fabric as you stitch.

You will be able to pin this seam for quite a long way keeping it flat. As soon as the seams start to part, stop pinning.

Go to the top of the seam and start to pin as before.

You will probably be able to put in two or three pins flat. Then, as with the bottom of the seam, the two edges start to part company.

Easing the excess.

2. Easing the excess

Now the interesting part of the seam starts.

If you look at the task in front of you it seems almost impossible, as the side body looks a lot fuller than the centre front panel.

This fullness forms the three-

Snipping the centre front seam.

dimensional shape that makes the jacket fit your body at the bustline.

3. Snipping the centre front panel
On the centre front panel make a few snips into the seam at right angles. As long as you don't snip beyond the 1.5cm (⅝in) seam allowance you can snip as many times as is necessary.

Do two or three snips first and ease the layers to see if the seam is long enough. Be cautious, as you are weakening the seam every time you snip. When you put the two edges together now, the snips will open up, enabling you to pin and sew the panels together easily.

As you are doing this pinning, be sure that the two edges of the pattern are still

---

HELPING TO EASE THE EXCESS

If you find that the top panel of the jacket is moving down as you sew, put your index finger between the two layers of cloth and put a small amount of pressure on the underneath piece of cloth. Don't put too much pressure on it as you will stretch the cloth out and distort the seam. If the seam starts to pucker too much when you are stitching, put some pressure on the seam at the back of the machine foot.

---

together at the edge. It is very easy to let them drift away from each other. A drifting seam will alter the fit of the jacket.

4. Side body to side front
Now sew the seam joining the side body to the side front.

This is a very straightforward seam and the two pieces should fit together neatly. Be sure to match the top and the bottom of the seam.

5. Centre back seam
The centre back seam is then stitched. If your pattern doesn't have a centre back seam, you can skip this process.

6. Centre back to side back
Follow the instructions for snipping the seam as for the centre front panel to side front.

You won't need as many snips as you did for the front seam because there is not as much shaping on the back as there is for the front.

Now you have the body of your jacket in three pieces: one back piece and two front pieces.

You don't need to join any more of the seams around the jacket yet as you will be putting the pockets in first and if all the panels are joined together it will make this process harder. The smaller the pieces you are working on the easier it is to sew; there won't be lots of fabric pulling at the pockets whilst you stitch.

Other seams that will need stitching are the short seam (forearm seam) of the sleeve.

As you pin this seam you will notice that the upper sleeve is about 6mm (¼in) longer than the under sleeve.

This extra fabric goes back to the original block pattern from which your pattern is drafted. On a block pattern there is a dart in the middle of the sleeve seam, to allow for the fullness required so that you can bend your arm when wearing the garment.

Instead of sewing out the dart in the

jacket sleeve, the extra fullness is the 6mm (¼in) difference in the seam lengths.

7. Stitching the forearm seam
Pin the seam with the under sleeve on top.

Match the top and bottom of the seam, encouraging the extra fabric into the middle.

As you stitch the seam the fullness should work its own way along and ease itself in.

8. Centre back seam of the under collar
This is the last seam on the main fabric of the jacket.

Pressing the Seams

You now need to press the seams open. I like to do my pressing in three steps, as outlined below. I use a steam iron and it's a combination of the steam and the heat of the iron which gives a good press on the seam. If a seam is pressed properly it should just disappear into the background of the jacket.

1. Pressing flat
Press the seam flat. This will set the stitches and get rid of any puckers that have occurred whilst machining.

Lots of people, when looking at the seam to be pressed, see some puckering on the seam and remove the stitching, adjust the tension on the machine and re-stitch the seam. However, the same

Pressing the seams, step 1, pressing flat.

Before I press seams, I use a spare piece of fabric, with a seam sewn in it, to test how much pressing the fabric will take. This will tell me if the fabric shines when being pressed. If it does, I need to use a pressing cloth for the seams.

The pressing cloth I like to use is silk organza as described in Chapter 1. You can press with a hot iron on this fabric without damaging it and it has the added benefit that you can see through the cloth, so you don't press any creases into the panels as you go.

This test will also show how much pressure I can exert on the seam before the seamlines start to show through. You definitely don't want tramlines on the seams of the jacket.

thing will probably happen again so don't worry about it too much at this stage.

All seams, whatever fabric they are made from, will have a little bit of a wobble on the edge. Press the seam flat before you start unpicking the seam;

Pressing the seams, step 2, pressing open.

nine times of out ten the puckers will disappear.

2. Pressing open

Use the point of the iron only, with some steam, and run the iron right along the seam.

When you get to a shaped part of the seam place the panels over a tailor's ham.

Make sure you are pressing the seam open smoothly. You can, with some fabrics, press along the seam just as I have said but then find that you have a ridge along either side of the seam when you turn it over to the right side. Take your time and make sure the seam is flat before you press it open.

3. Finishing the pressing

Turn the seam over to the right side. Unless you now press from the right side of the fabric you will finish up with a very homemade appearance to your jacket.

I usually use my silk organza pressing

Pressing the seams, step 3, final press.

When you are pressing the shaped seams open the tailor's ham will be especially useful. If you lay the seam over the ham it will fill out the shape, so that you can press without putting creases into the panels.

cloth over the fabric for this stage; this will prevent any sort of shine occurring on the fabric. Once you have a shine on the fabric it is almost impossible to get rid of, so prevent it from happening.

If you have a look at the seam from the right side, it has a very sharp pressed-open look down the middle of the seam but either side of it there is a small ridge, almost like a furrowed field. You need to remove the furrows.

Take the weight of the iron in your hand and, using steam and the pressing cloth, move the iron from side to side pressing either side of the seam flat. You don't need a lot of pressure to do this: it's more about smoothing out than pressing.

Once you are happy with the pressing of the seam, turn the jacket to the wrong side again. Check along the seam allowance to see if it's lying flat.

If the seam is starting to rise up again, snip into the seam allowance; this will create a bit of ease in the seam to help it lie flat.

Don't snip into the seam unless you are sure it needs it, because when you snip the seam is slightly weakened.

Press the clapper side of the point presser and clapper onto the seam once you are happy with it. You don't need to press hard: you are just trying to absorb the steam to set the seam in place.

This is contrary to the way most people see this tool. In the workrooms this tool is known as a banger. Many frustrations of the day have been taken out by using this tool with the banger name in mind, but it isn't really necessary.

When you are pressing open the short sleeve seam, pay particular attention to the first stage of the pressing. You have some fullness in this seam: by steaming the seam flat, you will shrink out the fullness.

Joining the Lining Panels

Now turn to the lining. You need to stitch all the body panels together. Start with the extra front panel you created, then continue with the side front, side body, side back and centre back.

Press all these seams open.

When you are pressing the lining seams, only use steam for the first part of the pressing process. Some linings can wither up or shine if you use too much steam. Always check that the lining can be pressed on the right side without making it shine before you turn it over. Shiny linings are not attractive.

When you make your own jacket, you get the chance to personalize it at several stages: the lining is one of them. I know that you will probably be the only person to see inside your jacket, but I like to decorate the insides of mine. There are two main ways of doing this: the first is to pipe the edge of the facing and the second is to embroider the lining.

Of course, you don't need to do either of these; just machining the front facing to the lining looks very professional.

Piping the Front Facing

If you are intending to put piping along the front edge of the facing, now is the time to apply it. You can either buy a ready-made piping or make your own. I'm going to use a ready-made piping for this jacket.

If you are making your own piping, there are a couple of things to bear in mind. Don't use a fabric which is too heavy; I like to use a lightweight satin or silk. Depending on the fabric and piping cord you are using, you may need to put a lining underneath the outside fabric because sometimes the ribs of the piping cord can show through a fine fabric.

Whatever combination you use, note

that cord does have a habit of shrinking. Before using it, put it on to the ironing board and steam it: sometimes you can see it shrink in front of your eyes. Always pre-shrink before cutting.

Making your own covered piping

1. Cutting the strips

If you are making your own piping you need to make sure that you cut the bias strips for the covering the cord at a 45-degree angle. By doing this, when you

Piping, step 1, cutting strips.

Piping, step 2, joining the strips.

cover the piping it will fit smoothly around the cord without puckering.

Mark your piping using tailor's chalk. I make my strips 3.8cm (1½in) wide. It is easier to work with a strip which is wider than you are going to need; cutting the strips narrower makes it fiddly to make whereas you can always trim off excess.

2. Joining the bias strips together

Machine the bias strips together so they

are long enough to fit the front facing. When you join them, lay right sides together and allow for a seam allowance of 6mm (¼in). The two strips will form a right angle on the inside edge (top right and bottom left in the photograph). Make sure you position the seam so you have the pointed part of the cut sticking out; these points can be trimmed off after you have stitched the strips together. Once you have joined all the pieces together to create a continuous strip, press open the seams.

This can be quite a confusing process, but I check every time by pinning the strips together, then laying the strip out flat, as if the strip has been sewn together, to see if it is joined correctly. This saves a lot of unpicking.

3. Covering the piping cord

Once the strips are long enough you need to machine them in place to cover the piping cord. Stitch the bias strip reasonably close to the piping cord using a zipper foot, leaving a little bit of ease between stitching and cord.

This is so that when you are machining the piping cord to the facing you can get a row of stitching in between the fastening row and the piping cord. You won't be able to see the first line of stitching once the cord is in place.

If you are lining the piping cord, this needs to go around the piping cord first, then place the fabric over it.

You don't need really thick piping

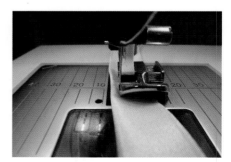

Piping, step 3, covering the cord.

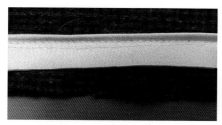

Piping, step 4, sewing the piping to the facing.

Piping, step 5, sewing the facing to the lining.

cord for this job. I usually use a size 1 cord as a maximum width but I sometimes use Austrian blind cord instead of the conventional cotton piping cord; this is a fine cord and gives a crisp effect but, again, pre-check for shrinkage.

4. Sewing the piping cord to the facing

Trim the edges of the strips covering the cord down to around 1cm (⅜in). Machine the piping cord onto the edge of the facing, so you are sewing right next to the cord on the 1.5cm (⅝in) stitching line. I prefer not to pin the cord, as it is easier to adjust it as you machine if it's not pinned down, but if you find it easier, then use pins.

5. Sewing the facing to the lining

Now sew the front facing to the front panel edge of your lining, using a zipper foot to get in close to the piping cord. When you press this seam, it needs to be pressed flat so that the seam edges point towards the lining, keeping the facing flat.

Your whole body lining should now be in one piece.

6. Sleeves

Finish by stitching both the sleeve lining seams. These seams need to be pressed flat, not open.

Alternative Decoration for the Lining

A good alternative to putting a piping trim on the facing to decorate your lining is to embroider it, providing you have an embroidery machine capable of doing this. With the exception of the sleeve lining pieces, all the lining body pieces need to be joined together and pressed as before, including the facing. I like to position my embroidery so it goes over onto the facing, but don't put it too close to the front edge as you will be cutting off excess fabric on this edge

and it would be a shame to cut into the embroidery. Make sure you use a stabilizer under the lining.

I like to use this method of trimming the lining as you don't see it normally but if the wind blows the front of your jacket open it is visible to the world. Of course, you will see it every time you put your jacket on and, just like wearing beautiful underwear, it will make you smile. I've used all sorts of pictures on the insides of my jackets: be inventive!

LOOKING AFTER WHAT YOU HAVE SEWN

Put the lining over a hanger and keep it hung up until it is needed. Use more hangers for the main panels, sleeves and under collar of the main fabric. You have just spent a lot of time pressing; don't crumple the pieces or you will finish up pressing again.

Chapter 6

The Pockets

Putting in the pockets is the next stage of making the jacket, and one of the joys of making your own jacket is that you can choose the style of pocket.

One of my favourites is the jetted flapped pocket. On a man's jacket this has a top and bottom jet, but on a woman's jacket it only has a bottom jet (the flap forms the top jet).

I like the smoother appearance of the flap instead of the top jet: it makes it more feminine.

It is a good idea to sew a practice pocket on a spare piece of fabric before you tackle the ones on your jacket.

On the jacket I've been photographing I'm going to put the jetted flap pocket in, but so that you have a choice of pocket I'm going to show you several styles you might want to use. I've used a tweed fabric for this and a different coloured thread to make it easier for you to see the stitching lines in the photographs.

On the list of things you need for a pocket, I have given you the choice of lining or cotton pocketing for the pocket bag. I prefer to use the former for my pocket bags but the cotton pocketing is a bit stronger, as the cotton is tightly woven. If you are going to put a lot of things into your pockets the cotton would be the better choice.

I don't like large pockets on my jackets unless it's an outdoor jacket or coat where I want to carry things like gloves, phones and so on.

Most bought patterns will have a 15cm (6in) pocket marked. This is far too large for most women; I usually make my

pockets around 12–12.5cm (4¾ –5in) at the most.

Remember that you have to cut into the front of your jacket for the length of the pocket, so making a longer pocket disrupts the front of the jacket more than a shorter one.

It's up to you whether you want a straight or slanted pocket.

Preparation

Marking the pocket position

Using the tailor tacks marked on the front of the jacket as your guide, draw a horizontal straight line with tailor's chalk. (I have assumed for the sake of simplicity that the pocket is gong to be straight rather than slanted.)

Whichever pocket you are doing, make sure that the front line of the pocket is parallel to the centre front.

Mark the front of the pocket with a vertical line crossing the position line of the pocket and about 2.5cm (1in) in front of the princess-line seam.

Measure the length of the pocket you require and put a second vertical line through the pocket position.

Once you have marked one front pocket position, place the other jacket front on to the table. Lay the marked front on top of it.

Making sure you have placed the pieces this way round, check that both fronts are aligned exactly, one on top of the other. Gently bang the place where

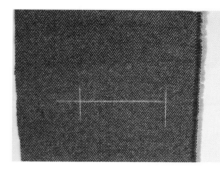

Pocket markings.

Strengthening the pocket.

the chalk line is: this will transfer the pocket mark through to the second front. It is bound to be in exactly the same place on each side.

If you have placed the pieces upside down, you won't get the chalk marks coming through: you can't defy gravity! Check the marks on both fronts to make sure that the chalk lines are clearly visible; re-mark if necessary as banging the chalk through will probably make the original line faint.

Strengthening the pocket

For all the following pockets, you will need to put a strip of fusible interfacing on the wrong side of the fabric where the pocket is positioned. This layer of interfacing will add strength to the pocket.

Cut a piece of Washable Supersoft (medium-weight) interfacing 5cm (2in) wide, making sure it is longer than the size of your pocket by 2.5cm (1in) at each end. Fuse the interfacing into place on the wrong side of your fabric so that the pocket position is in the middle of the interfacing strip.

Applying interfacing

By following the next three steps you will be able to stick the interfacing into place without it coming away from the fabric later on.

Make sure the interfacing doesn't hang over the edge of the fabric. This is to stop the interfacing from sticking to your ironing board. If this happens, when you pull away the interfacing it will leave some glue on your ironing board. This could get stuck onto your iron or your jacket if you iron over it again.

The following instructions apply to the Washable Supersoft interfacing I have recommended. Other interfacings will have their own method of application; follow the manufacturer's instructions.

1. Shrinking the interfacing
You need to shrink this interfacing before you apply it to the fabric. Lay the interfacing to the wrong side of the piece it needs to be applied to. Hover the steam iron over it and put lots of steam over the interfacing. You may see it shrink in; this doesn't always happen, but you will see little bubbles appear all over the interfacing. Take the interfacing off the fabric.

2. Positioning the interfacing
Place the interfacing back on the fabric in the correct position. Put the iron gently onto the interfacing and apply a small amount of steam and heat to it.

The interfacing will not stick properly at this point. This process is only to position the interfacing at the correct place. At this stage you can peel the interfacing off the piece if it's not positioned correctly.

3. Fusing the interfacing
Fuse the interfacing into place by putting the iron onto the interfacing, applying a jet of steam and then counting slowly to ten. It's the combination of steam and heat which melts the glue making the interfacing stick. Let the piece dry before you test to see if the interfacing is stuck.

Test to see if the interfacing is stuck by pulling the piece on the cross grain and listening. If the interfacing is stuck, you won't be able to hear anything. If you can hear crackling, the interfacing is not stuck.

If it crackles, just go back to the iron and apply a bit more heat and steam for a bit longer.

Jetted pocket completed.

Jetted Pocket

Bring out the stock of fabric left after cutting the main pieces of the jacket.

For each jetted pocket you will need:
- For jets: 2 pieces, each 20 cm (8in) x 5cm (2in) in main fabric, the longer side following the straight grain
- **For pocket back:** 1 piece 20cm (8in) x 7.5cm (3in) in main fabric, the longer side following the straight grain.
- **For pocket bag:** 2 pieces, each 20cm (8in) x 20cm (8in) in lining or cotton pocketing.

PRECISE CUTTING FOR JETS

Before cutting, find a thread on the straight grain that's slightly longer than the cut you want (here 20cm/8in). Fray the edge out so that the chosen thread is left exposed and then trim off the frayed part of the fabric. I also mark each piece I've cut with a chalk cross on the wrong side, so I know instantly which is the right and wrong side of the fabric whilst I'm making up the pocket.

Making up the jetted pocket

1. Machining the first jet into position
Place one of the jets up to the edge of the chalk line. Make sure it is in the middle, with some fabric over the ends of the pocket at either side.

Machine from one end of the pocket to the other using a narrow seam. I usually use 6mm (¼in). Don't machine this seam too wide, or it will make a very chunky-looking pocket.

Jetted pocket, step 1, machining first jet.

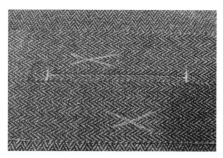

Jetted pocket, step 2, marking for second jet.

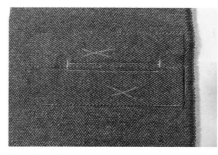

Jetted pocket, step 3, positioning second jet.

Jetted pocket, step 6, pressing the pocket open.

To make a neat pocket, start and finish exactly on the chalk line. A smaller stitch is recommended, a 1.5 instead of a 2.5 normal length.

Make sure you have a couple of reverse stitches at the beginning and end of the jet to stop it coming undone.

2. Marking the pocket position on the second jet

Using tailor's chalk, mark each end of the pocket onto the jet you have just stitched.

This seems as if you are repeating what you have already done, but once you place the second jet into position ready to machine, your chalk line will be underneath the jets and you won't be able to see the start and finish marks exactly.

Make sure you have a very sharp piece of chalk so that the ends are definitely marked where they should be. A blunt piece of chalk can leave a mark up to 3mm (⅛in) wide. Although this doesn't sound like a large amount, the extra couple of stitches required to get to the edge of the chalk mark can make the pocket look very lop-sided.

This is where a chalk box comes in very handy (see Chapter 1 for details).

3. Positioning the second jet

Butt the second jet up to the first and machine it in place as for the first one, starting and finishing exactly at the chalk lines.

4. Sewing one side of the pocket bag

Machine one piece of the pocket bag lining to the bottom jet.

Jetted pocket, step 4, first side of pocket bag.

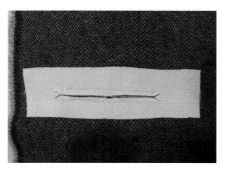

Jetted pocket, step 5, cutting though the pocket.

Place the lining underneath the jet, right sides together, and machine a small seam, using the edge of the foot as your seam guide.

5. Cutting through the pocket

Now the scary bit. You need to cut the jacket front through the middle of the jets. Stop 6mm (¼in) away from each end and then, keeping the jet out of the way, mitre into the corners. You need to snip as close as you can get to the stitching line.

You need to be brave about this because if you don't go right into the corners you will finish up with a very strange corner to your pocket.

6. Pressing the pocket open

You are now going to press open the small seams holding the jets in place on the pocket.

Start with the lower jet and pull the lining up towards the top of the jacket; this will start the opening process.

Press gently along the length of the jet using the tip of the iron. Use the wooden clapper to absorb the steam and set the seam before you move on to the top jet.

Pull the top jet through the middle of the pocket via the opening you have just cut.

By doing it this way, you won't crease up the bottom jet when you are pressing the top one open.

Press open the top jet and use the clapper as before.

Press the lining seam, keeping the jet flat.

7. Basting the jets in place

Turn the jacket to the right side and push the bottom jet through to the wrong side.

Using a single basting thread, baste the two jets in place, filling the gap you created when you stitched the jets.

Jetted pocket, step 7, basting the jets in place.

Make sure both sides of the jets are an equal width.

Pay particular attention to the ends of the jets; the pocket must have square ends.

Position the basting stitches just below the jets because by placing the stitching here it will be out of the way when you machine.

Don't baste beyond the end of the pocket as you need to get underneath the pocket for the next stage.

8. Stitching out the ends of the pocket

Lift the jacket front out of the way so you can see the pocket underneath.

This should reveal the triangle of fabric which you created when you mitred into the corners of the pocket.

Lay this piece of fabric flat on top of the basted jets.

Stitch close to the edge of the pocket though the triangle: this will secure the ends of the pocket. This is quite a tricky

Jetted pocket, step 8, stitching out the ends.

process, so take your time and get it positioned correctly before you start to machine. It can be quite delicate if you have to unpick this stitching line. Repeat at the other end of the pocket.

9. Stitching the bottom jet into place

Turn the jacket front over to the right side. Machine in the ditch of the seam along the bottom jet.

If you are not confident about stitching in the ditch, you can do this process by hand, but it is much stronger if you do it on the machine. This row of stitching should be invisible from the right side of the fabric.

10. Positioning the back of the pocket

Take the second piece of the pocket bag lining and lay the pocket back onto it, keeping the top edges together.

At the bottom of this strip of fabric, come up 1.3cm (½in) from the bottom and snip into each side of the pocket bag. Turn the fabric piece upside down so the top edge matches the snips. Right sides of the fabric should be together.

Stitch a 6mm (¼in) seam to attach these two pieces together.

Turn the pocket back up, towards the top of the pocket bag, and press it flat.

Attaching the pocket back in this way eliminates the need for neatening off the edge of the fabric, which can be a little bulky.

This piece is now pinned in place at the back of the pocket. The fabric should be in the middle of the gap where you

Jetted pocket, step 10, positioning the back of the pocket.

Jetted pocket, step 11, machining the top jet.

put your hand into the pocket. This will ensure that you won't be able to see any lining when the pocket is finished.

11. Machining the top jet in place

On the front of the pocket and starting at the bottom corner of the jets, machine level with the stitching line holding the bottom jet in place, then turn and continue across the top jet and down the other side, to finish at the bottom corner. Again, this line of stitching should not be visible.

12. Replacing the basting

Before you move on to making up the pocket bag, remove the rows of basting stitches along the jets. Replace them with a row of oversewing so that the basting stitches draw the two jets together.

GAPING JET POCKET

If your pocket looks as if it's going to gape, move and pin the top jet down, closing the gap before you stitch, not the bottom jet up. If necessary, overlap the top and bottom jets slightly. The top jet is fixed in place with the machining line; the bottom jet is free to move so you can use the pocket. Your instinct will tell you to move the bottom jet but don't: this is a common mistake.

Jetted pocket, step 12, replacing the basting.

Flapped pocket completed and ready for final press.

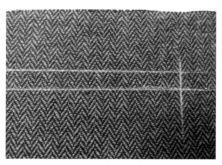
Marking the flapped pocket.

13. Machining the pocket bag

Fold in the edges of the pocket bag close to the end of the machining.

Run a fingernail along these folds to make the crease sharper. Do the same at the bottom, marking the pocket to the depth required.

If you want to, mark these lines in chalk to make it easier to see whilst you are machining.

Machine all round your pocket bag on the lines drawn. When you get to the bottom sew round corners, not square ones: this will stop dust collecting in the corners of your pocket. Trim off the pocket lining leaving a 1cm (3/8in) seam allowance.

Now give the finished pocket a good press. Absorb the steam using the point presser: this will set the pocket in place. Pressing the finished pocket now makes it easier as you don't have any interfacings or linings getting in the way. The pocket is also flat.

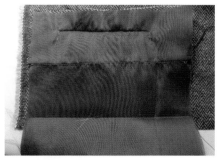
Jetted pocket, step 13, machining the pocket bag.

Flapped Pocket

For each flapped pocket you will need:

- For jet: 1 piece 20cm (8in) x 5cm (2in) in main fabric, the longer side following the straight grain.
- For pocket back: 1 piece 20cm (8in) x 7.5cm (3in) in main fabric, the longer side following the straight grain.
- For flap: 1 piece main fabric, Washable Supersoft (or comparable) interfacing and lining, cut as detailed below.
- For pocket bag: 2 pieces, each 20cm (8in) x 20cm (8in) in lining or cotton pocketing.

This pocket is made in a similar way to the jetted pocket with the exceptions outlined below.

When you have marked the line for the pocket position, mark a second line 1.3cm (1/2in) above the first one.

This will be the line you stitch the flap to.

You need to mark the end of the pocket at the front. Mark the back of the pocket as before; this is just a guide. The flap has to be made first to check the length of the finished pocket.

Fuse a piece of interfacing on the wrong side of the fabric as for the jetted pocket.

1. Cutting the flap

Cut out two pieces of main fabric for the flaps. I usually lay a spare piece of cloth over the pocket position and then transfer the chalk marks onto the flap.

This will make certain that the flap is cut at exactly the same angle as your pocket, whilst keeping the flap on the straight grain of the fabric.

To check that you have the marks of the pocket in the correct position, lift the edge of the flap up and down quickly: if you can't see any difference between the front panel and the flap, you have it placed properly.

The two marks at the ends of the horizontal line will be the finished sides of the flap at the top edge. It's up to you as to how deep you want to cut the flap:

I usually cut mine to finish around 6.3 cm (2½in) deep.

If the fabric is quite heavy, it might be better to cut them a bit deeper, so they hang without sticking out.

When you measure the bottom edge of the flap, make it 2mm (1/8in) wider at the back of the flap than the top edge.

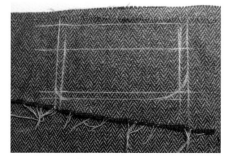
Cutting the flap.

This may seem like a strange thing to do, but when you put the jacket on and the pocket goes around your body, it creates an optical illusion that the flap is slanting in. By leaving the extra on the bottom of the flap, it stops this from happening.

The seam allowance on the sides and bottom edge of the flap is 6mm (¼in).

The top of the flap has a 2.5cm (1in) seam allowance; this will be stitched inside the pocket.

You could leave your flap with square corners if you want to, but I prefer to round off the bottom corners.

On the front corner of the flap you could use any round object you have to hand, such as a pin tin or a coaster. Place your round template onto the bottom of the flap and draw round it with sharpened tailor's chalk. Trim the flap off to this line.

At the back of the pocket, you don't need such a rounded shape, so you can just snip off the corner and make it into a rounded shape by eye.

Make sure both the flaps are cut exactly the same.

If you are cutting a flap with patterned fabric, such as a check or stripe, you will need to lay the fabric for the flap over the position of the pocket and match the piece of fabric exactly to the jacket front. If you match the flap exactly, you shouldn't be able to see the piece for the flap clearly when you half-close your eyes: it should just disappear into the front of the jacket.

If there is a seam or dart running through the pocket, you won't be able to match it all the way along: you match the bit of the flap nearest to the front of the jacket.

This is because this is the part of the pocket which will be seen clearly. Your arm will obscure the rear of the pocket when you are wearing the jacket.

Mark the position of the pocket onto the fabric. You can then remove the fabric piece and cut the flap to shape as described above.

Another possibility is to cut the flap on the cross grain instead; this could be a great design feature on the right fabric. If you are doing this, the lining and interfacing for the flap are cut on the straight grain of the fabric, giving stability to the flap and stopping it stretching out of shape whilst you are making it up.

Whichever option you have chosen you need to cut a piece of lining fabric and a piece of interfacing the same shape as the flap.

I like to use a fusible interfacing on the back of the flap. As mentioned for the jetted pocket, the interfacing I use is called Washable Supersoft. It is a woven interfacing, so you cut it on the same grain as the flap. (This is the same interfacing that I use for strengthening the back of the pocket.)

You can use lightweight tailoring canvas and hand-stitch it in place, then use an edge tape to finish off the edge of the canvas, but I find this quite bulky for a lady's jacket.

2. Making the flap

Apply the fusible interfacing to the wrong side of the flap (see the instructions at the beginning of the chapter).

With wrong sides together, sew the lining to the flap, pulling the lining slightly tight as you sew. This will help to keep the lining from showing around the edges when the flap is turned through to the right side.

Leave the top edge open for turning.

When finished, turn the flap right sides out.

Baste round the edge of the flap, rolling the lining inwards slightly. Press the flap flat, using the point presser to absorb the steam; this will set sharp edges on the flap.

3. Marking the pocket

Mark the depth of the finished flap in tailor's chalk on both sides of the flap. If the pocket position on the jacket front has become a little blurred whilst you have been cutting the flap, re-mark both lines.

Re-mark the position of the front of the pocket if necessary. If you are using a patterned fabric, make sure the flap is still matching at the front.

4. Marking the edge of the pocket

Place the flap on the top line, making sure the front of the flap is on the line marking the front of the pocket.

Use the flap to mark the rear of the pocket. Tip the chalk to the underside of the pocket before marking it; this will make sure the flap is not too big for the

Marking the edge of the pocket.

Making the flap.

Machining the jet in place.

pocket.

5. Machining the jet in place

Place the jet so it is next to and positioned centrally on the lower line you have just marked.

Set the stitch length on your machine to 1.5. Machine the jet in place along this line, using a 6mm (¼in) seam allowance.

Take care to start and finish exactly on the chalk lines either side of the pocket.

Machine one piece of the lining bag to the other edge of the jet, placing right sides together and using the edge of the foot as your seam allowance.

6. Machining the flap in place

Stitch the flap to the top line by turning the flap upside down and machining along the line marked. You will be stitching on the lining side of the flap. Make sure this line is directly on top of the line marked on the jacket front.

As you have marked both sides of the flap, this should be easy to do by lifting the flap and checking frequently that one chalk line is on top of the other as you machine.

7. Cutting through the pocket

Cut through the pocket, keeping the flap out of the way. Stop 6mm (¼in) away from the ends of the stitching.

Cut mitres into the corners, keeping both the flap and the jet out of the way. Be brave and cut right up to the stitches.

8. Pressing the pocket

Pull the lining bag towards the top of the jacket and, using the point of the iron, press the seam with the jet open.

Machining the flap in place.

Pressing the flapped pocket.

This is done in the same way as the jetted pocket. Only the point of the iron is used so that you don't crease the flap whilst it's lying in the wrong direction.

Then lay the flap flat into its finished position and press again. Also press the seam of the pocket bag, keeping the jet flat.

9. Basting the jet into place

Position the jet up so that it fills the gap left between the stitching line and the flap.

Baste into position. This will make the jet wider than on the jetted pocket.

Complete the pocket by following the instructions for the jetted pocket from step 8.

Basting the jet into place.

Welt pocket completed.

Welt Pocket

This pocket is traditionally used as a handkerchief pocket on a man's jacket, but you can use it as a side pocket on both jackets and coats for ladies. This style of pocket is usually horizontal along the front, but you can turn it to be vertical or at an angle. I like to use this style when I'm making coats, as it can be cut quite large without any gaping.

For each welt pocket you will need:

- **For welt:** 1 piece 8.1cm (3¼in) x length of pocket, plus two seam allowances in main fabric, the shorter side following the straight grain.
- **For pocket bag:** 2 pieces, each 20cm (8in) x length of pocket, in lining or cotton pocketing.
- **For welt interfacing:** 1 piece 3.8cm (1½in) x length of the piece above for the welt, in Washable Supersoft interfacing.

1. Marking the pocket position

Mark the position of the pocket as before,

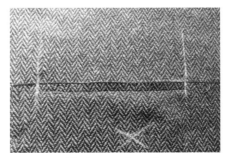

Machining the welt.

with a positioning line and the two ends. Extend the latter above the pocket so that they are the width of your finished welt.

Fuse a piece of fusible interfacing to the back of the pocket to strengthen it, as with the previous pockets.

2. Machining the welt

Position the welt fabric piece to the bottom of the marked line, right sides of the fabrics together.

Machine the welt to the bottom of the line, using the edge of the foot as your seamline and making sure you go exactly from one chalk mark to the other.

Re-mark the ends of the pocket onto the welt. This may seem like a strange thing to do, but you are going to cover up the original chalk line with the lining being stitched on: if you don't re-mark the lines you won't easily be able to see where to start and stop the stitching line holding the lining in place.

3. Stitching the lining in place

Butt one of the lining pieces up to the stitched edge of the welt on the other side of the chalk line. Stitch in place, starting

Stitching the lining in place.

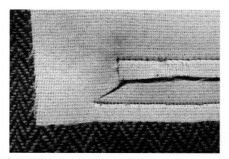

Cutting the pocket open.

and finishing 6mm (¼in) short of the marked line at each end. Again, use the edge of the foot as your seam allowance. This piece of lining will be the back of your pocket and form one side of the pocket bag.

Place the other piece of lining to the edge of the welt, right sides together, and stitch in place using the edge of the foot as your seam allowance. This piece will be the other side of your pocket bag.

4. Cutting the pocket open

Fold the pocket in half, making sure the two stitching lines are one on top of the other.

Make a snip through the middle of the two lines. Open out the pocket and continue to snip along this line in both directions.

Stop when you are level with the finish of the stitching line on the lining. Snip into the seam on the lining, cutting through both the jacket front and the lining.

Keeping the welt out of the way, cut a mitre into the corners of the pocket on the bottom seam.

Make sure you cut right into the corner or you won't be able to press the pocket open properly.

5. Strengthening the welt and pressing

Fuse the interfacing to the wrong side of the welt piece, following the instructions listed for the flapped pocket.

Turn the jacket front over so you can press open the seam of the welt. Pull the welt towards the top of the jacket. This will start the opening process for pressing the seam.

The lining, which is attached to the welt, needs to be pressed down so that the welt is flat.

The side of the lining which is stitched to the jacket will be pressed flat. Pull it through the opening for the pocket and down towards the bottom of the jacket before pressing.

6. Marking the welt

Mark in the finished width of the welt. I

Marking the welt.

usually use 3.1cm (1¼in) for a jacket, but you could go slightly wider or narrower. For a coat you could go up to 5cm (2in).

Turn the edge of the welt back so you can see the chalk mark underneath. Crease a line along the welt exactly where this line is, then mark the chalk line on the welt. This needs to be done at both ends of the welt.

The finished shape of the pocket is now clearly marked onto the welt.

Basting the welt.

7. Basting the welt

Turn in and baste the two short edges, and along the top edge of the welt. Make sure the two ends are folded in before you baste along the top edge.

Make your basting sit no more than 6mm (¼in) from the edge. You are going to turn in the fabric at the back of the side edges and if you baste too deep it will be impossible to do this.

Basting the back of the welt.

8. Basting the back of the welt

Position the welt so you can see the piece to be folded in and the seam in front.

Snip the back of the welt in line with the machined line, to the edge you have just basted into position.

Open out the fold to continue snipping to the edge of the lining if necessary. It needs to be snipped in far enough that you can turn it in neatly.

The back of the welt needs to be positioned so the turning sits neatly at the back of the welt. You don't want to see this side of the welt when the pocket is

Hand stitching the welt.

finished. Baste the ends in place. Push the lining attached to the welt through to the wrong side of the fabric.

9. Hand-stitching the welt

Start your hand-stitching on the inside of the welt, at the top of the right-hand side.

Fell stitch in place until you get to the machined line at the bottom, then bring the needle through to the right side of the pocket and prick stitch in the ditch from one side to the other.

When you get to the other edge of the welt, bring your needle through to the wrong side and fell stitch up to the top of the welt.

The welt is now all finished off ready for stitching down to the jacket front.

If you are working on heavyweight fabric, you might want to give the welt a good press to flatten it out before you move on to the next stage. Use the point presser to set the welt.

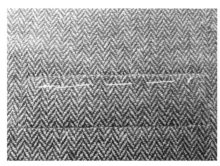

Stitching the sides of the welt.

10. Stitching the sides of the welt

Now fell stitch the welt into place along the sides, extending your stitches for 6mm (¼in) along the top edge of the welt on both sides.

Remove all the basting stitches holding the sides in place.

Put in another row of basting across the top of the welt, going through the front of the jacket as well as the welt: this basting line will keep the pocket in the correct place whilst you stitch the pocket bag.

11. Stitching the pocket bag

Finish the pocket bag as for step 13 on the

jetted pocket.

Give the pocket a final press.

Fully lined tailor's patch pocket.

Fully Lined Tailor's Patch Pocket

For each patch pocket you will need:

- **For patch:** 1 piece in main fabric; see steps 1 and 2 below for details.
- **For lining:** 2 pieces, each 20cm (8in) x 20cm (8in), in lining or cotton pocketing.
- **For back interfacing:** 1 piece 7.5cm (3in) x 20cm (8in) in Washable Supersoft interfacing to strengthen the back of the pocket).
- **For interfacing:** 1 piece 5cm (2in) x 20cm (8in) Washable Supersoft Interfacing for the facing of the patch pocket.

This is probably the hardest of the pockets to master. I can't stress too much how vital it is to get the preparation right. The stitching of this pocket is fiddly, and almost impossible if the preparation isn't right.

It is worth all the effort, when you put your hand into the pocket at the end.

Take your time and enjoy making this beautiful pocket.

1. Cutting and preparing the patch

Cutting out the pieces for this pocket and the preparation of the patch need to be as accurate as possible.

Decide where and how big you want

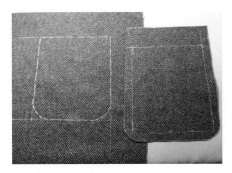

Cutting and preparing the patch.

your finished pocket to be. I usually use a finished size of about 13cm (5in) x 15cm (6in) or bigger. Don't try to cut it much smaller or you won't be able to stitch it on.

If your fabric has a pattern, you will need to cut the patch as for the flap on the flapped pocket instruction, matching the pattern precisely.

This pocket will look terrible if you don't match the pattern but if you get the matching right you will have to look twice to see it on the jacket when finished.

Using tailor's chalk, mark the finished pocket size on the jacket front.

When you mark the pocket you need to make sure that the front edge of the patch is on the straight grain of the fabric of both jacket and patch.

The bottom of the patch needs to be 2mm (a bare ⅛in) wider than the top. This is because, when you wear the pocket, it goes around the body and creates an optical illusion that the bottom goes in.

Thread trace the shape of the pocket on the jacket.

Again, make sure you are accurate with the stitching, as this will be the line you are following when you stitch the patch on.

Fuse a piece of Washable Supersoft interfacing onto the wrong side of the jacket panel, positioning it so that the top edge of the patch is in the middle of the interfacing.

This will strengthen the pocket and stop it from stretching outwards when you put your hands into it.

2. Cutting the patch pocket

Lay the fabric for the patch over the thread-traced line. If you need to match a pattern, make sure that the fabric is in the right place.

Mark in tailor's chalk exactly the same size pocket onto the patch.

You will need to add seam allowances to the patch: 3.8cm (1½in) on the top edge of the patch, 1.3cm (½in) around the rest of the pocket. Round off the bottom corners of the pocket, making sure both corners are cut to the same curve.

You don't need any fancy tools for drawing the rounded corners of the patch: use a pin tin or a drinks coaster to mark it, just as for the front of the flap on the flapped pocket.

3. Setting the top edge of the patch

Fuse the Washable Supersoft interlining to the seam allowance at the top of the patch. Then press in the 3.8cm (1½in) seam allowance to create a facing.

Join one piece of the lining to the facing edge of the pocket using a small seam.

Press the lining towards the bottom of the patch; this piece of lining will line the patch pocket.

Fold in a seam allowance of 1.5cm (⅝in) at the top edge of the second piece of lining. Place this onto the wrong side of the patch; the two layers of lining will be right sides together.

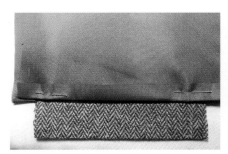

Setting the top edge of the patch.

Preparing the patch pocket for stitching.

Lay the top edge of the second piece of lining so that the folded edge is level with the seamline of the patch pocket.

Pin into place.

4. Preparing the patch pocket for stitching

Machine round the raw edges of the patch, keeping all three layers flat.

You will need to stitch from the right side so that you can follow exactly the shaped edge of the patch.

The second layer of lining will line the jacket, inside the pocket.

Carefully trim the lining to the same size and shape as the patch, which is now ready to attach to the jacket front.

5. Marking the balance marks for stitching

Place the made-up patch onto the jacket front so that the folded edge at the top is on the straight row of thread tracing.

Marking the balance marks for stitching.

Make sure it is exactly where the finished pocket should be.

You need to have balance marks all round the patch: you can't use the usual methods of marking (snipping the points or tailor tacks) as you won't see them once you start to sew. Instead, using tailor's chalk, mark straight lines along the sides and bottom of the pocket and extend the line to the outside of the pocket and onto the jacket.

Make sure you put a line through the rounded corners of the patch at the bottom.

Remove the pocket from the jacket front. Re-mark the chalk lines, transferring them onto the back of the patch pocket.

Extend the balance marks on the jacket so that they are visible in the middle of the area where the patch is to be positioned.

6. Stitching the patch in place

You are now ready to apply the patch pocket to the jacket.

Place the patch on the left-hand side of the marked pocket position. Place the patch so that the edge is up to the stitching line and the balance marks match. You are sewing a 6mm (¼in) seam.

This needs to be accurate or the pocket will pull tight or be loose once it's stitched all the way round.

Inside the pocket, stitch all round the patch, keeping the edge of the pocket to the thread-traced line and the balance marks in line. You will be inside the patch pocket as you go round.

If you get to a place where the balance marks don't match, *stop*. There is no point in continuing as the pocket will be askew when you complete it. Just unpick a little bit of the stitching until the balance marks match, then continue sewing. You may need to put some pressure onto the jacket front as you stitch to stop the patch pocket moving out of line.

Take your time when you are stitching this patch into place. It is easy stitching the sides of the pocket, but you will have to ease the corners in to make them fit.

7. Setting the lining

Give the pocket a press, to make sure everything is sitting correctly. Then lift the top of the patch pocket out of the way to reveal the edge of the seam allowance at the top of the patch.

Reinforce the side of the pocket by stitching inside along the edge of the seam and then continue to stitch across the top of the lining and up to the top of the pocket seam on the other side. Fell stitch the patch for 6mm (¼in) on either side of the patch to cover the seam allowance.

Now test out the pocket. It has a rewarding feeling when you put your hand inside this pocket as you can't feel any rough or raw edges.

Once the pockets are complete, join the side seams of the jacket. The body of your jacket will now be in one long piece, just the same as your jacket lining.

You can now put away all the spare pieces of cloth you have. I like to roll them all up into a bundle and tie a piece of cloth around them to keep them neat and tidy. If they are all secured together they are much easier to find if you need any more pieces later on.

In the tailoring trade, these spare bits are called cabbage or mungo. When they have enough scraps the mungo man comes to take them away for recycling.

Re-marking the balance marks.

Stitching inside the pocket.

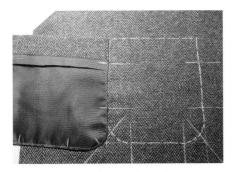

Stitching the patch in place.

Setting the lining.

Chapter 7

The Foundations of the Jacket

If you employed a builder to build you a house and he or she said, 'I don't think I'll bother digging out the foundations as the ground seems quite solid,' would you employ them? A jacket needs foundations inside it to stop the fabric collapsing whilst you are wearing it; also the fabric needs shaping to get it to lie as you want it to do. There are several stages to achieving this, the first one being the canvasses.

The main canvas is put right through the front panel piece and extends into the underarm and shoulder area just like a giant T shape. The canvas provides support for all the most important parts of the jacket, starting with the front edge where you will work the buttonholes. It continues up through the lapel area (which will need to be worked into shape), along the neck edge (where the collar will sit) and into the armhole (to provide support for the sleeve).

These are the most important parts of the jacket. When you meet anyone the sleeves and the collar form a frame around your face, where the person speaking to you will be looking. You don't want a sagging collar or a pleated sleeve to let you down.

There is an extra section placed on the top of the canvas; this is called the plastron.

The plastron area on a jacket is the area which covers the shoulder, running along just inside the break line, and it extends into the armhole area as well.

To explain to students the reason for having this piece I usually say, 'Imagine putting one end of a ruler onto your

shoulder and the other end onto your bust point. In between these two points there will be a gap underneath the ruler. The plastron fills this gap and pads out the jacket to stop any collapsing of the jacket front when you are wearing it.'

The word 'plastron' comes from a suit of armour, where it denotes the breast plate that forms extra protection around the chest area. You, of course, don't need a metal plate inside your jacket but several layers of different fabrics are used. This T shape also creates extra protection for the area on top of which the sleeve and collar sit.

For a lady's jacket I don't put any canvas into the back of the jacket as it can be very heavy and restrict movement.

Cutting the Canvasses

The following measurements are the ones I use for a standard jacket. Depending on the shape of the person the jacket is for, you might want to cut the canvas or plastron area slightly larger or smaller than these measurements.

For instance, if you are making the jacket for a woman with a large bust, you might want to make the plastron a bit smaller, but you might want to cut an extra layer to it, as the gap between the shoulder and the bust could be bigger than on a lady with a smaller bust.

The T-zone

If you are adding extra layers to the T-zone, make sure you graduate the edges of the canvas. You don't want a ridge around

the edge of the layers, as this would show through the jacket.

To cut the canvasses for your jacket you will need the patterns for the centre front, side front and, if your pattern has one, a side body.

1. Cutting the centre front

Start the pattern for the canvas by looking at the centre front; all of this panel is cut in lightweight tailoring canvas.

Now lay the side front and the side body beside the centre front. Mark a point about 10cm (4in) below the armhole on the side seam or below the dot on the side body. Gently curve a line from this point towards the edge of the centre front panel. **Note:** Do not draw a straight line at this stage. Our bodies are all a series of curves; drawing a straight line will mean that you will see the canvas edge more readily through the jacket.

Make yourself a new pattern using the line you have just drawn as the bottom edge of the pattern piece.

Keep the straight grain line the same as the original pattern on the side front panel.

2. Cutting the side body panel

Once you have cut the patterns as above, look at your pieces.

If your pattern has a side body (as shown here) you can lay the small side body piece against the side front piece. There is very little shaping in this seam, so remove the seam allowance on both pieces, butt the edges up to one another (be careful not to overlap them) and tape the pieces together.

If you find there is a lot of shaping on this seam and it is impossible to join the two pieces together by butting the edges

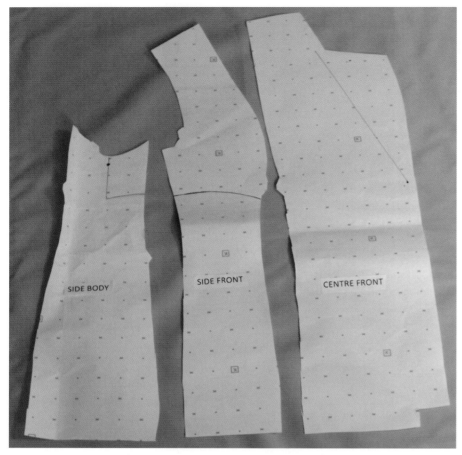

Cutting the T-zone, step 1.

Lay the two pattern pieces side by side.

Draw in a line 1.3cm (½in) away from the break line; this line is on the jacket side of the break line, not the lapel side.

Mark in a point 3.8cm (1½in) above the break point. Then mark in a point 7.5cm (3in) below the armhole at the side nearest to the underarm.

Join these two points in a slow gentle curve to form the bottom edge of the new pattern.

Remove the seam allowance from the neck edge. You can now cut both pieces for this layer from chest canvas.

5. Cutting the top layer of the plastron

The third and final layer is cut almost the same as the chest canvas layer, except that you remove 1.3cm (½in) from the bottom of the pieces. This means that when you lay all the canvasses together you will have a graduated edge to them: if you cut them all the same, you would have a ridge.

This third layer is cut from domette.

If you make a pattern piece for each of these layers, you will always have it whenever you make a jacket, so you won't have to cut the pattern again.

Making Up the Canvasses

Once all the layers have been cut, they need stitching together. First, lay the lightweight tailoring canvas for the centre front onto the tabletop.

Make sure you have the right side of the canvas down onto the table; you should be able to see the pencil line for the break line. Check that you have a right-hand side and a left-hand side.

Then place the chest canvas on top of these pieces, matching the shoulder and armhole edges.

Finally, lay the domette on top of the chest canvas. Make sure you keep all the layers together as you stitch.

together, cut separate pieces and make two joins in the plastron.

3. Cutting the other pieces

Now lay the pieces for the princess-line seam together, centre front to side front starting at the top. You will see that the pieces won't fit together in a straight line as the other seam did. It looks as if there is a dart missing from the bottom of the pieces. This is correct. Once you sew the two edges together, you will get the shape for the jacket front.

You now need to remove the seam allowance from the side body panel along the princess-line seam. Then remove the seam allowance on the centre front panel downwards for the length of the side body panel.

The reason for removing the seam allowance for the princess-line seam is that you can't join canvasses and press seams open as you would ordinary fabric. The canvas is too heavy to press open and would just keep springing back up and not lie flat.

Both pieces of this layer of the T-zone are to be cut in lightweight tailoring canvas. Mark the break line on both sides of the centre front canvas using a pencil; do this on the wrong side of the canvas.

4. Cutting the first layer of the plastron

The pattern for the first layer of the plastron is cut using the canvas pattern you have just made.

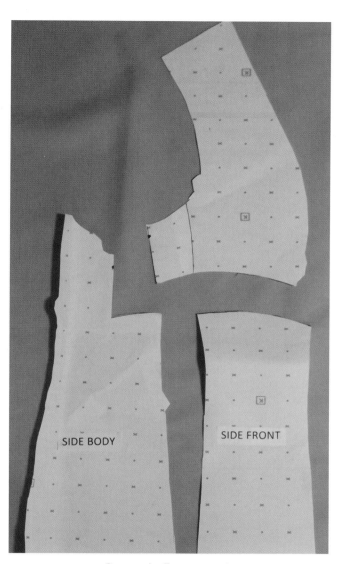

Cutting the T-zone, step 2.

SIDE BODY

SIDE FRONT

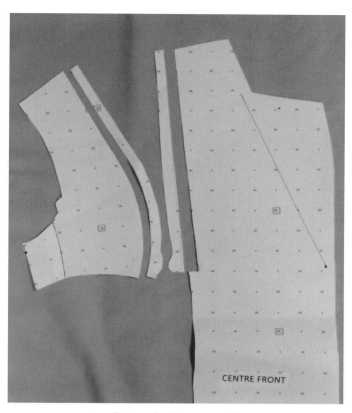

CENTRE FRONT

Cutting the T-zone, step 3.

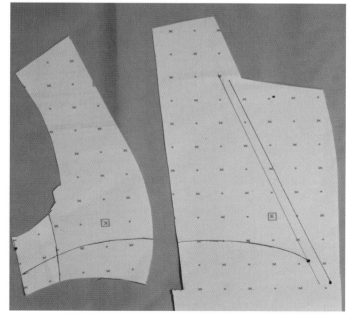

Cutting the first layer
of the plastron.

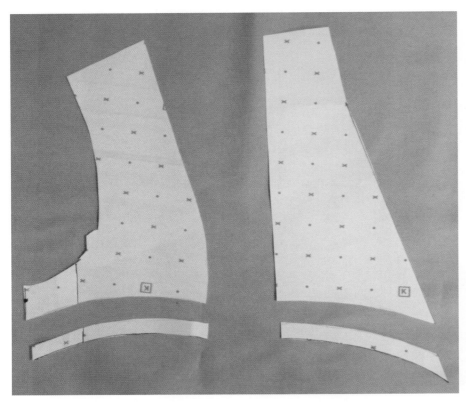

Cutting the top layer of the plastron.

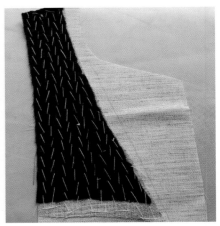

Completed pad stitching.

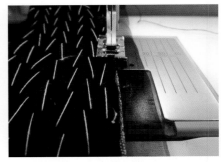

Shaping the canvas, adding the joining strip.

Shaping the canvas, joining the panels.

Pad stitching

Using the instructions for this stitch as detailed in Chapter 1, follow the directions for the flat form of this stitch. I would recommend that you use a thimble to do this. It is the ideal opportunity to get used to using the thimble if you haven't done so before. No one will see these stitches so if they are not quite as neat as you would like, it doesn't matter. Your sewing may be quite slow and the thimble will seem as if it's getting in the way to start with but you will get faster as you get used to it.

Your fingers will be very sore at the end of this padding if you don't use one.

This stitching may seem a little excessive, covering the whole of the piece, but it does need to be done. If you just stitched around the outside edge of the pieces, which would be the logical thing

to do, it would hold the pieces together whilst you made up the jacket but the second you started moving about when wearing the jacket the three layers would move independently of each other. The canvasses, being a heavier weight than the domette, would start to wear through and the whole T-zone would be useless.

You need to repeat this process for the side body panels on both sides of the jacket, positioning the layers in the same sequence as described for the centre front panels.

Joining the canvasses

Now you need to join the side front of the canvas to the centre front. I use a strip of silk organza to do this job but you could use a piece of lining if you don't have the silk organza. As long as it is a lightweight

fabric that doesn't shrink when it's pressed, it will work.

Cut a strip of silk organza 3.8cm (1½in) wide by slightly longer than the length of the pieces you are joining together. You will be trimming off the excess fabric at the end, but it is easier to work with a slightly wider and longer piece when machining.

1. Making the shape in the canvas
Place the edge of one side of the canvas in the middle of the silk organza strip. Using a straight stitch, machine as close to the edge of the canvas as possible.

When you get to the bottom, butt the next panel up to the edge of the first one and again stitch as close to the edge as you can.

Make sure the two edges stay together all the way along; don't let them overlap or part in the middle forming a gap.

By doing this you will make the shape in the canvasses as if you were joining the seams or making a dart.

The shaping will now be exactly the same as your main fabric shaping, but you will find that it's quite easy to pull the stitching of the join apart.

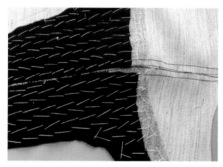
Strengthening the join.

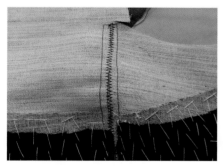
Tidying up the raw edge.

2. Strengthening the join
Machine around the join again, this time using the edge of the machine foot as a seam allowance; this is measured from the joining edge of the canvas.

This row of stitching will make the join much stronger and therefore less easy to pull apart.

If you look at the join you will find that the edges still stick up, and it looks very rough.

3. Tidying up the raw edge
Adjust your machine to a zigzag stitch, making the width of stitch as wide as the machine will allow. The length needs to be between 1 and 2.

Machine over the join in the canvas: this will make a smooth finish to the seam.

Trim off any excess silk organza, both along the length of the join and at the top and bottom. Press the canvasses where the seam is, using a tailor's ham to keep the shape. You have done a lot of work to get the shaping into the canvas, so press carefully using the ham all along the seam.

4. Covering the edge of the chest canvas
I find the edge of the chest canvas is too rough at the bottom of the canvasses. To stop this causing a problem, I cover the edge using a fusible off-grain tape. This is easily ironed onto the canvas, using heat and steam to stick it into position.

To position the tape, place the middle of the off-grain tape over the edge of the

Covering the edge of the chest canvas.

canvas. Because the tape is off-grain, you should be able to shape it around the bottom of the canvas easily.

You will need to stitch this tape down as well, as it will move as you wear the jacket and could come away from the canvas. I use a large herringbone stitch to secure it to the canvasses.

Basting Out

The next part of the making-up process is split into two separate stages. The first one, where you attach the canvasses, mark up and get everything perfectly trimmed and ready to put on the facing, is called basting out.

The second stage, when you have the facing machined on, and you are fastening everything, including the lining into its final position, is called basting under. Both of these processes are done before you stitch the shoulder seams, whilst the jacket is still flat.

Canvassing the jacket

The first step is to fasten the canvasses to the jacket. Lay the canvas on the table so that the plastron is facing the tabletop and the smoother side of the canvas is uppermost, where the jacket front will be.

I like to work with the front lying with the shoulder nearest to my right hand. Whenever I start to baste, I always start at the top of the jacket, which can be easily smoothed down to adjust if necessary.

Put the wrong side of the jacket on top of the canvas; the right side of the cloth should thus be on top. Match the seams and make sure that all of the areas which need canvas behind them are covered.

Check the centre front, lapel, neckline, shoulder seam and armhole edge to make sure the canvas is in the correct position. If you gently pat the jacket, you will be able to tell if everything is lying correctly. If anything feels lumpy, smooth the

Basting the first row.

Cutting the canvas.

Pulling the pocket through the canvas.

Basting the second row.

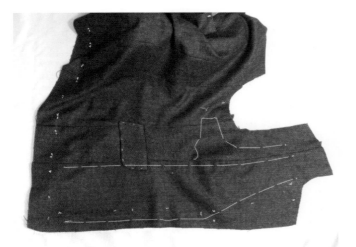

Basting the third row.

main fabric along the canvas to make it lie in the correct position.

Using basting thread, you are going to stitch three rows of basting stitches to hold the canvas in place. These stitches need to be about 5cm (2in) long. As you start or finish your basting lines, make sure you leave about 7.5cm (3in) to the top and bottom of the jacket. A slightly smaller measurement 5cm (2in) applies around the armhole and neck edge. This space is needed so you can get inside to machine the shoulder seam later and have access to get inside all the other edges.

Basting the first row; securing the middle of the canvas

Starting 7.5cm (3in) below the shoulder edge, baste the jacket to the canvas using the princess-line seam as your guide. You need to put the stitching just in front of this seam, until you get to just above the pocket. As you baste, keep checking that the canvas is still lying in the correct position.

Leave the needle in the jacket and turn the jacket over.

You need to cut a piece out of the canvas so that you can pull the pocket through and behind the canvas. This will enable you to fasten the pocket bag to the canvas and when you press the front of your jacket there will be no pocket edges showing through on the right side of the garment.

Cutting the canvas

Cut the canvas just above the stitching line holding your pocket in place until you see the end of the pocket.

Then cut a line parallel to this cut about 1.5cm (⅝in) below. Now cut through to the first line so that you can remove the small oblong of canvas.

Pulling the pocket through the canvas

Pull the pocket bag through the slot you have just cut in the canvas. Lay the canvas behind the pocket so it is flat on the wrong side.

Turn the jacket back to the right side and make sure that you lay the jacket flat again. Ensure you also get the pocket bag flat. Continue with the basting line, following just in front of the princess-line seam until you get to 7.5cm (3in) above the hemline. Stitch through the pocket bag as you go.

Finish the row of basting with a back stitch.

Basting the second row; securing the armhole edge of the canvas

The second row of stitching is to secure the armhole edge of the canvas. Start 7.5cm (3in) below the shoulder and 5cm (2in) in from the armhole edge. Baste around the armhole edge until you get to the underarm. Work a back stitch before you change direction.

Then, feeling the edge of the canvas underneath, baste near to the edge of the canvas, down under the arm and across to join up with the first row of basting on the princess-line seam.

Basting the third row; securing the front edge of the canvas

Starting at the top of the break line and stitching 1.3cm (½in) inside the line, baste the full length of the break line to the top buttonhole. Stop basting 2.5cm (1in) before the front edge. Make a back stitch before changing direction to go down the front of the jacket.

Now baste downwards 2.5cm (1in) from the edge of the fabric. This will allow you to trim off the edge without cutting through this row of basting.

As you go down, ease in a small amount of fabric towards the princess-line seam.

The amount is about 2mm (bare ⅛in). You should be creating a little bubble of cloth between the row of basting you are doing and the first row of basting along the princess-line seam.

Finish this line of basting just above the hemline.

You are easing the fabric in at this point to give a roll to the front edge. Put your arm underneath the front of the jacket and let it drape around you. The fabric should now be nice and smooth. Your arm is acting the same way that your body will whilst you are wearing the jacket. If you don't allow this extra, you could finish up with the front edges 'dog-earing' upwards when the jacket is finished.

Marking up and preparing the front and lapel

1. Marking up the front for pad stitching

You are now going to set up the front of the jacket ready to pad stitch the lapels. You will need a very sharp piece of tailor's chalk.

Draw in the top button/buttonhole position, extending this line out to the front edge.

Now draw another line parallel to this line and 1.5cm (in) above it. The distance between these two lines will eventually become the transition between the front of the jacket and the lapel.

If you can't imagine this, think of a jacket facing. From the bottom of the jacket up to the break point it sits on the inside of the jacket. Above this point it becomes the lapel and sits on the outside of the jacket. Because fabric has some depth to it, it can't immediately turn over. So this gap in between the top button and the second line enables the fabric to roll over smoothly.

Now mark in the 1.5cm (⅝in) seam allowance from the front edge of the jacket, in between the two lines marked horizontally.

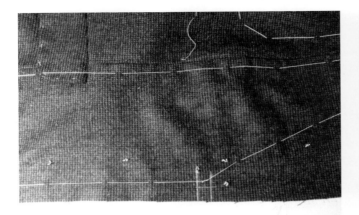

Marking the front for pad stitching.

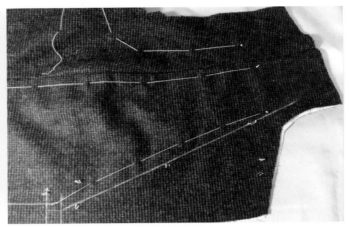

Marking in the break line.

2. Marking in the break line

Go to the neck edge of the jacket at the top of the break line. Mark in the 1.5cm (⅝in) seam allowance.

Mark a line to join this mark to the point at which the top horizontal line and front edge cross (the break point). This is the break line.

3. Thread tracing the break line

Thread trace this line in place. This is done by a row of basting with stitches about 2.5cm (1in) long with a tiny stitch in between (which makes the stitching line look continuous). You will be basting through the canvas as well as the main fabric.

Remove the tailor tacks marking this line, as they are no longer needed.

4. Adding a layer to the lapel

Cut a piece of cotton fabric (I usually use a piece of cotton lawn). The fabric is cut as an oblong, which needs to be slightly longer than your break line and slightly wider than the width of your lapel at the top, with the straight grain of the fabric running along the long edge.

The break line on the jacket is slightly off straight grain because of the way the jacket is cut; that is, the front edge is on the straight grain. You need to prevent the break line from stretching out whilst you are working on it: this piece of fabric will

enable that process.

Position this cotton piece in between the canvas and the jacket fabric, as close to the break line as possible. Baste into place 1.5cm (⅝in) from the break line. Then trim off any excess fabric from the edges once it is basted into place.

5. Adding the bridle

Cut two pieces of lining on the straight grain of the fabric, 5cm (2in) wide x the length of the break line plus 10cm (4in). This piece of lining is known as the bridle.

Its job is to make sure that the break line doesn't stretch out whilst you are working on it or when you are wearing the jacket.

It will reinforce the piece of cotton you

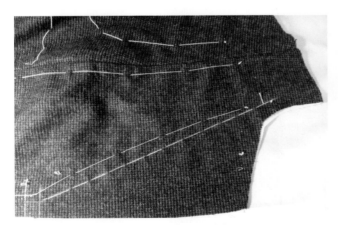

Thread tracing the break line.

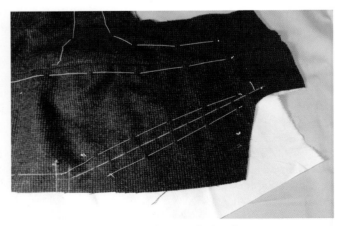

Adding a layer to the lapel.

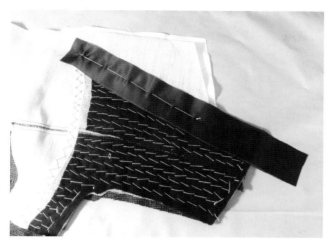

The bridle.

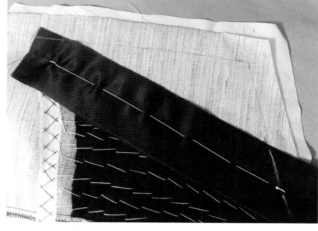

Marking the area to be pad stitched.

put in between the fabric and the canvas.

Turn the jacket over to the wrong side, so you can see the canvasses.

Baste the middle of the bridle over the line of thread tracing marking the break line.

Make sure that there is no ease in this piece of lining.

6. Marking the area to be pad stitched

To mark the area you need to pad stitch, measure in 2cm (¾in) from the edge of the main fabric, along the top of the lapel and all along the edge of the lapel at the front edge. I like to use a pencil for marking this area, as tailor's chalk will wear off when you start to stitch it.

The pencil line will not be seen when the lapel is finished.

Mark both fronts exactly the same.

7. Pad stitching

The pad stitching is worked in the same way as you did when you padded the canvasses, except that the stitches and rows need to be much smaller. The stitch length is 1cm (⅜in) and the rows are 1cm (⅜in) apart. Use the thread with which you are sewing the seams of the jacket, not basting thread.

8. Stitching the bridle

Start the stitching at the inside edge of the bridle (the edge furthest away from the front of the jacket). From this edge until you get to the basting line in the middle of the bridle, you will be stitching with the lapel flat and just attaching the stitches through the bridle to the canvas.

9. Rolling the lapel

Once you get to the middle of the bridle, you need to curl the lapel over, as if it were sitting in its finished position, and stitch right through to the right side of the lapel.

You should be able to see tiny dots of stitches on the right side of the fabric. As you stitch further out towards the edge of the lapel, keep rolling it so the place you are stitching is always right on the top of the roll.

10. Finished padded lapel plus pocket bag

By rolling the lapel in this way the bottom layers of the lapel will naturally shorten as you stitch. The lapel will stay curled once

you have finished. When the lapel is made up it will naturally lie back, making a beautiful line on your finished jacket.

As you stitch out towards the front of the jacket the lines of stitching will get shorter due to the shape of the lapel. Don't stitch beyond the pencil line you have marked.

Rolling the lapel.

Stitching the bridle.

Finished padded lapel.

You can now fasten the pocket bag to the canvas. Use a large slip stitch to fasten the outside edges of the pocket bag down to the canvas only. Don't go through to the main fabric.

Doing this will stop the pocket from getting creased or puckering up during wear.

Application of the facing

Most people who have a problem making jackets say that they have difficulty with either the collar or the sleeves. By following each of the next few stages you should eliminate these difficulties.

There are four elements to making the collar: the facing, the under collar, the top collar and the process of drawing the collar pieces together.

You won't actually be putting the collar on for quite a while yet, but the facing needs to be in place before you start work on the collar.

As you work through the collar stages, check at every step to make sure that the jacket is sitting beautifully, and don't move on until you are happy that the process in hand is perfect. By treating each stage separately and perfecting it before moving to the next, you should get the collar on without any tears.

Marking and stabilizing the front edge

The next stage of this process will seem as if you are repeating the marking-up of the lapel before pad stitching it. In some ways you are. The reason for doing it again is because of the pad stitch shaping.

The process of working the stitches can distort where the break line is. By re-marking it you can make sure that it is in the correct place; this time you will be thread tracing the break line right through to the bridle.

My students find this stage of tailoring

a bit disconcerting as they have never looked at making a jacket in this way before. Sometimes it looks as if you are trimming quite a lot of fabric off, but if you follow the instructions, you will get a beautiful finish to your jacket.

This marking needs to be very precise. The shape you are drawing in will be the shape of your finished jacket front. Make sure you use a sharpened piece of tailor's chalk and a ruler. You may need to sharpen the chalk again before you mark in the second front.

1. Re-marking the break line

This process is the same as steps 1–3 of marking up the lapel for pad stitching.

Remove the basting holding the bridle onto the jacket, the basting holding the piece of cotton lawn in place and the line of stitches marking the break line.

Re-mark the following positions: the top button, the break point 1.5cm (⅝in) above it, and the seamline in from the front edge. The seamline should form a cross with the two lines going horizontally across the jacket.

Then re-mark the seamline at the top of the break line at the neckline. Join this mark to the break point. This will be the new break line.

Thread trace this line as before. By re-marking this line, you have checked that everything is still in the correct position; if it became distorted whilst you were pad stitching, you have corrected it. Redoing the thread tracing will enable you to see

Marking in the hemline.

the break line clearly through the bridle on the wrong side of the garment.

2. Marking in the hemline

Go to the bottom of the jacket and mark in the hemline of the jacket by joining up the tailor tacks, but only on the centre front panel to start with. Where the hemline runs into the front edge you should make sure that it forms a right angle. Remove the tailor tacks once you are happy with the hemline marking.

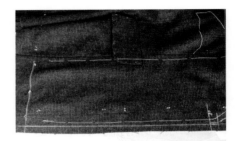

Marking the front edge.

3. Marking the front edge

This next step is the one which scares my students when they start, but it's a matter of preparation and practice. You are going to trim the seam allowance down to 3mm (⅛in). By using a small seam allowance, it enables you to be more accurate when stitching the facing onto the jacket.

At the break point mark in 1.3cm (½in) from the raw edge. Then go to the bottom of the jacket front and mark in 1.3cm (½in). Join these two marks with a straight line. Make sure you use a ruler.

You may notice on the front edge that your jacket has distorted by quite a large amount. Don't worry; it only moved about because you have been sewing and pressing it. That's the reason you are shaping everything up before you sew on the facing.

If you remember, right at the beginning of the toile-making stage of this jacket, I cut the front edge with a straight finish to it.

Marking in the rounded jacket front corner.

Now is decision time; do you want to keep the square corner at the bottom front of your jacket or make it rounded?

4. Marking the rounded jacket front corner

If you want a rounded shape here, the shape once it's made up must merge smoothly into the bottom edge of the jacket.

When you mark this shape, start by marking a line 3mm (⅛in) below and parallel to the marked hemline.

Take a circular object. I usually use a pin tin or drinks coaster but if you want a more dramatic shape, use something bigger. Place it so that the edges of the tin (or coaster) sit right onto the front edge mark and the line you have just drawn in below the hemline mark. Draw in the front shaping.

Once the shaping reaches the line marked just below the hemline, mark a line going straight down to the edge of the jacket at the bottom.

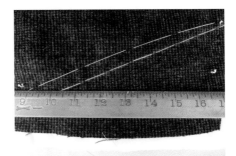

Marking in the lapel shaping.

5. Marking in the lapel shaping

You now need to mark the front edge above the break point.

Go to the top of the lapel and mark in 1.3cm (½in) from the edge of the fabric at the top of the lapel.

You need to join this mark to the seam allowance already marked in where the top buttonhole is.

If you place the ruler between these two marks you will see that the lapel is shaped, and it is not a straight line.

I use a lapel shaper to mark this line in.

The top edge of the lapel is easily marked in. Go to the magic dot and mark in a line going straight up to the edge of the fabric.

Lapel shaper in position.

LAPEL SHAPER

This is just a piece of cardboard cut to the shape of a lapel. It is easier to use this shaper as you only have to line up the top and bottom of the lapel to get the correct shape.

There is a pattern for a lapel shaper at the back of the book. If you draw round it and then cut the shape out in card, you will be able to mark up your lapels without any problems every time you make a jacket.

Marking in the top of the lapel.

You are now going to put two marks in to form the top of the lapel, both of them 1.3cm (½in) from the edge of the fabric. The first one is where the magic dot is, the second is at the outside edge of the lapel. Join these two marks in a straight line.

Once you have marked in this line, you can remove the tailor tack at the magic dot.

6. Trimming off the edge

Now trim off along the lines you have just drawn, starting at the magic dot at the top of the lapel. Snip into the cutting line, then continue across the top of the lapel, along the length of the lapel to the break point, down the front edge, around the shaping at the bottom of the jacket and stop when you get to the hemline, then remove the whole piece by cutting down to the bottom of the jacket.

7. Marking in the second front

Following the instructions for steps 1 and 2 above for marking in the first front, mark

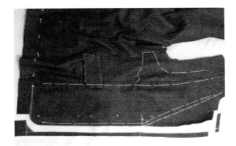

Trimming off the edge.

Marking in the second front.

Trimming the canvas.

Securing the edges of the jacket.

in the second front of the jacket. Make sure you can clearly see the chalk lines.

Place the first front on top of the second front. Check that the break line, top button, side seam and hemline are perfectly matched. Then draw in the edges of the second front, using the first front as a pattern.

Trim off the second front as before.

By doing it this way you can be certain that both fronts are exactly the same shape and size.

8. Marking in the hemline
Mark in the rest of your hemline so that you have a continuous chalk line joining up the lines previously marked on the two centre front panels. The line going around the bottom won't be completely straight, as it follows around the shape of the body. You can draw a curved line around this bottom edge. You will need to use a ruler to get this line drawn accurately (see the box below), then thread trace the position of this line.

I like to trim the edge of the bottom of the jacket with pinking shears, as this can prevent any sharp hem finishes showing through from the right side.

Marking in the hemline.

DRAWING A CURVED LINE WITH A RULER

This can be done quite easily by having a series of marks to follow along the line. Mark in the hem allowance on the seamlines. Place the ruler on the starting mark. Keep your eyes on the next mark along the hemline and gradually move the ruler towards it as you draw in the line.

This does take a bit of practice but can be achieved. Don't look at the point at which you are drawing: this will probably result in a straight section in the curved chalk line. You can apply these same rules to drawing in all sorts of curves.

9. Trimming the canvas
You now need to trim back the canvas inside. Remove 3mm (⅛in) from the edge of the canvas, all round where you trimmed the edges.

You can remove the canvas from the hemline as well. Trim this so that you leave 1.3cm (½in) below the hemline. You should be able to measure where this line is from the thread tracing.

Note: You will be removing all the seam allowance from the canvas. This will create a guideline for stitching when sewing the facing in place. It also means that you won't be stitching through canvas on the edges of the jacket. It is difficult to press canvas flat once it has been stitched through.

10. Securing the edges of the jacket
To secure the edges you have just cut, you need to put some edge tape on to stop them fraying out. In gentlemen's workrooms they traditionally used a linen stay tape hand-stitched to the edge. I find this tape very bulky for ladies' jackets and instead use the same fusible off-grain tape used to finish off the edge of the canvas at the bottom of the plastron.

Because it is cut 13 degrees off straight grain it acts as a stay tape but has enough give to let you go round the shape of the front edge without distortion.

Applying the tape is really easy; you just need heat and steam.

The tape needs to be fused exactly on the edge you have just trimmed, from the hemline at the bottom of the jacket to the magic dot at the top of the lapel.

Work your way around the edges of the jacket, sticking the tape to follow the shape of the jacket. At the corner of the lapel, mitre the tape and continue along the second side.

If you have a rounded shape to the bottom of your jacket, you will need to pull the tape slightly taut as you fuse it. This will make the edge roll towards the

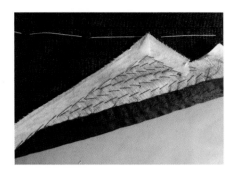

Fastening the tape.

inside when the jacket is finished.

The inside edge of the tape will be on the canvas, the outside edge will be on the jacket fabric only.

11. Fastening the tape
You need to fasten the edge of the tape which is fused to the canvas. Using a single thread, slip stitch the edge of the tape to the canvas. Do not stitch through to the main fabric.

12. Pressing the break line
Press along the break line, creasing the lapel exactly along the line of thread tracing you put in earlier. You will need to be able to feel this line when basting the facing into place. Use the point presser to absorb the steam when pressing the break line in.

13. Positioning the lining
Always work with the top of the jacket to the right-hand side. Don't keep turning it:

it will stay much flatter if you don't move it too much.

Lay the jacket onto the table, right side uppermost.

Lay the lining on top of the jacket so that you have right sides together.

Position the lining, matching the side seams.

Check that the lining is 1.3cm (½in) over the edge of the jacket at the armhole edge. (You cut this extra around this edge when you cut out the lining.)

Check that you have lining covering the shoulder and the rest of the armhole.

Place a line of pins down the side seams to keep everything in place.

Smooth the lining out towards the front of the jacket but be careful not to pull the lining tight. At this point you are ignoring the back of the jacket.

You should have the facing covering the centre front with extra fabric hanging over the edge of the jacket. Don't try to match the front edges together.

This is probably totally alien to those of you who have never tailored anything before. Dressmaking patterns will always tell you to match everything along the seamlines. Here, you have allowed for extra fabric on the facing so that, if you need to, you can adjust it.

14. Basting the facing in place
Using basting thread, start to baste the facing in place along the break line. You

should be able to feel the ditch in the jacket where you creased the lapel.

When you get to the break line, do a back stitch to secure it (but don't break off the cotton).

Continue to baste along the front edge of the jacket. Again, you should be able to feel the edge through the facing.

As you baste, ease in a little fabric upwards. This will give you enough fabric spare when you baste the facing flat to stop the facing curling outwards, which would create a dog-eared corner. Break off the thread.

This time you will need to have some ease coming in from the edge.

You should be aiming to get a straight grain line running along the edge of the lapel. It is difficult to see this on a plain cloth, but if you have a stripe it should run as much as possible along the edge of the lapel.

The stripe running neatly along the edge of the lapel is one of the ways to recognize a good-quality, handmade suit.

15. Roll of the cloth
When you get to the top of the lapel, you will also need some fullness coming down from the top.

To check if you have enough fullness in your lapel, run your finger diagonally into the corner of the lapel. If you have a ridge of fabric around both sides of your finger, there is enough fullness to create the roll

Positioning the lining.

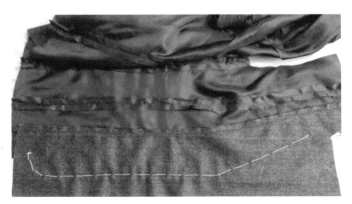

Basting the facing in place.

Roll of the cloth.

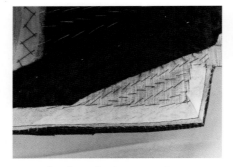

Stitching the facing in place.

Turning the lapel.

of the cloth.

This is the term used to describe the amount of fabric you need so that the seam sits underneath the lapel. When the jacket is finished, the seam should not be visible on the edge of the lapel.

You can now remove the basting thread holding the break line in place down to the back stitch at the start of the centre front.

By doing this, you can smooth the fullness out of the way temporarily whilst you stitch the facing in place. If you leave the fullness in the way, there is a chance that you could stitch a pleat into the corner of the lapel.

Repeat this section for the second side of the jacket. Make sure, as you lay the lining flat to baste the facing in place, that you haven't twisted the lining.

16. Stitching the facing in place
Make the stitch length on your machine a bit smaller than the average length; I prefer a length of 1.5. Using the 3mm (⅛in) seam you left when trimming the edge, stitch from the magic dot at the top of the lapel down the centre front and around to the edge of the facing at the bottom. Stitch so that you can see the jacket front on top.

You will have to start one front at the magic dot and the other at the hemline.

If you have a square corner at the front bottom of your jacket, just continue to the bottom edge.

When you get to the corner of the lapel,

make sure you stitch a square corner. Do not stitch across the corner: if you do it will never look square.

Basting Under

1. Trimming the edges
Remove all the remaining basting from the facing and take the pins from the side seam.

Trim the facing down so that it is 3mm (⅛in) larger than the jacket.

Snip into the magic dot, right up to the stitching line. *Do not* cut across the corner of the lapel.

Note: If you trim across the corner, it leaves only a very small amount of thread right where the corner is. In the way of things, by the time you have turned the corner through this thread will have perversely pulled itself through and will be sticking out on the right side of the lapel, which will ruin the look of the garment.

2. Turning the lapel
Most fabrics, when trimmed down to this size of seam allowance, will turn without difficulty but if your fabric is causing a problem, follow the next instruction.

To help you turn the corner of the lapel, take the jacket to the iron.

Fold one side of your corner over, wrapping the large side of the seam over the smaller side along the seamline.

Then repeat this with the other side of

the corner.

Holding the two sides where you have just folded them, press flat.

Be careful when pressing such a small area. Don't forget to remove your fingers before using the steam.

Now refold the corner and put either your fore finger or thumb (depending which lapel you are turning) inside the lapel. Open out the corner with your other hand and push the folded seam down inside the lapel.

Carefully turn the facing through to the right side. If you give a little wiggle to the corner, it should pop out as a perfectly square corner.

3. Basting the edges
You now need to baste the edges of the jacket, rolling the seam the correct way. To do this you need to make sure you know which way to stitch.

From the break point upwards, the seam needs to roll so the facing is on top.

From the break point downwards, it

Basting the edges.

needs to roll towards the facing side, as a normal facing would do.

Use basting thread for this job. Roll the seam so that you can see the seam on the side you are working from.

Start at the top of the left-hand lapel at the magic dot. You will be working from the wrong side of the lapel, facing underneath.

Making sure you have a knot in the thread, bring the thread through from the right side of the jacket close to the edge of the seam.

Then take the needle straight down from the edge by 1cm (⅜in).

Take a stitch about the same distance to the left-hand side. This will form a diagonal stitch on the right side of the lapel.

This stitch holds the edge much more solidly than a normal straight running stitch.

Work from the top of the lapel down to the break point.

Then go to the break point on the other lapel and work your way up to the magic dot. On both lapels, make sure you are working on the underside of the finished lapel. Roll the edges of the seam to get a good line whilst you are doing this basting.

Now turn your jacket round and work from the break point on the right-hand side of the jacket down towards the bottom, rolling the seam in the opposite direction; in other words, the seam should be on the facing side of the jacket. You will still be using the same stitch.

When you get to the hemline, use normal basting stitches to turn up the hemline along the thread-traced line you made earlier.

When you get to the bottom of the other side, switch back to the edge basting and work up to the break point.

Lining in

You are now going to start the process of lining in; that is, basting the lining in place. Doing it now whilst the jacket is still flat makes it much easier to do. I always carry out this process with it flat on the table.

1. Facing

Baste a row of stitches 2.5cm (1in) from the edge of the facing so it runs parallel with the row of edge basting you have just completed. As you stitch, roll the lapel back into its finished position and bring the facing up towards the lining.

At the bottom of the facing, you will need to turn in the seam allowance of the facing so that it sits flat with the bottom edge of the facing slightly to the inside of the jacket hemline.

Now stitch a row of basting 1.3cm (½in) in front of the break line.

Hang the lapel over the edge of the table whilst you stitch 1.3cm (½in) the other side of the break line. When you get to the break point, continue basting down to the bottom whilst putting your fingers under the front edge, tipping the front edge off the table.

This will ensure that the facing won't roll back onto the wrong side whilst you are wearing it.

On the second facing, you will have to baste from the bottom to the top.

The final row of basting on the facing goes along the edge where it joins to the lining. Start this row of basting in line with the lapel. Don't start at the shoulder edge, as you will need to get inside the jacket for the collar and the sleeves. (Refer to the photo where you can see my knots.)

2. Fastening the facing to the canvas

You now slip stitch the seam of the facing to the canvas inside.

Start stitching where the basting finished on the right side, using fairly large stitches about 1.5cm (⅝in) long.

When you get to where the pocket is, break off the thread. Continue from the bottom of the pocket until you get to the hemline.

3. Fastening the hem of the jacket

At the hemline, turn back 6mm (¼in) of the hem and continue to slip stich across the bottom and round to the facing on the other side. Sew up the facing, avoiding

Lining in.

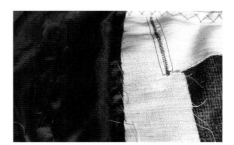

Fastening the facing to the canvas.

the pocket as before. Finish stitching at
the same point you started from on the
other side.

4. Setting the lining in place
Lay the jacket flat on the table again. You
are going to baste the rest of the lining
flat, working on each section at a time.
Don't try to flatten the whole jacket out at
once: it is impossible.

You need to leave at least 5cm (2in) in
from all the edges before you start to
baste. This is so you have enough room to
get inside the jacket to put the sleeves and
collar on: it is an advantage if you don't
have to remove these stitches to be able to
do that.

5. Fastening the front lining
Before you start to baste any of the
following lines, check to see if everything

Setting the lining in place.

Fastening the hem.

in the section is lying flat; I find that
patting the lining helps to get this right.

Starting with the front, baste around the
front armhole, leaving 7.5cm (3in) to the
shoulder and 5cm (2in) to the armhole
edges.

Backstitch when you get to the side
seam.

Continue to baste down the side seam,
stopping when you get to 5cm (2in) from
the bottom edge.

Backstitch again, then baste across the
bottom 5cm (2in) from the hemline until
you reach the facing.

Repeat this on the other front.

6. Lining in the back of the jacket
Start with the upper back lining above the
waistline.

Lay the back lining in place, making
sure the lining covers the armhole,
shoulder and neck edges of the jacket,
overlapping it by 1.2cm (½in) round the
armhole, shoulder and back neck edges.

The lining will be too big for the back.
Remember you left a 5cm (2in) pleat down
the centre back when you cut the lining
out.

Fold over the pleat so it sits on top of the
centre back seam.

The first row of basting goes across the
lining where the waistline of the jacket is.
Don't move the jacket to baste this line;
baste from side to side, keeping the pleat
in the centre back in place.

Starting 5cm (2in) below the neck edge,
baste the pleat down to the basting line at
the waistline.
Check to make sure the pleat is on the
centre back and that the lining hasn't
distorted and still overlaps the edges of
the jacket.

Now secure the rest of the top back
edges. This is a continuation of the first
line of stitching basted around the front
armhole edges.

Baste from the side seam around the
armhole edge, across the back neck, down
around the other armhole until you reach
the side seam on the other side.

When you have done this line of
stitching, the whole of the top of the lining
will be in place.

Now move the jacket below the
waistline so that the lining is flat.

Position the pleat so it lies on the centre
back seam. Double-check that there are no
bubbles in the back of the lining. Any
excess lining can be folded into the pleat.

Baste this pleat downwards to 5cm (2in)
from the bottom of the jacket. Then baste a
row of stitching going from one side seam
to the other, placing this 5cm (2in) above
the hemline of the jacket.

7. Basting the hem
The next step is to trim off the excess
lining from the bottom of the jacket.
Trim, leaving 1.2cm (½in) of lining below
the hemline.

I like to trim this by feeling where the
hemline is through the lining, but there is
nothing wrong with turning the jacket
over so you can clearly see the finished
hemline. It is safer to turn it over if you are
doing this for the first time. You don't
want to accidentally cut the bottom off the

Basting the hem.

Marking up the shoulder.

Setting the plastron.

jacket!

You will need to unpick some of the lining from the front facing as you need to be able to turn the lining independently of the facing.

Unpick the seam until you are about 3.1cm (1¼in) above the hemline. Turn the hem of the lining up, so that it is 2cm (¾in) above the jacket hemline. Baste in place, 1.3cm (½in) above the lining hemline.

A common mistake my students make when turning up the lining hem is to pull the lining too tight between the fold of the hemline and the row of basting going across the jacket 5cm (2in) above.

This mistake can sometimes go unnoticed until the jacket is finished and all the basting stitches are removed. It will look as if the bottom of the jacket is flicking up and won't sit flat.

One of the most common questions I'm asked when making jackets is about what to do with the raw edge of the facing. There are a couple of ways of finishing it off but the way I prefer is to cross-stitch it down; see full instructions under hand-finishing in Chapter 10.

Lightly press the bottom edge of the jacket to flatten out the lining, then press in the lapel and front edges.

Use the point presser and clapper once you have put steam into the edge; this will set the edge immediately.

Marking up the shoulders

Before joining the shoulder seams, you need to check the shoulders and armhole edges, just as you did when you marked up the front edges before you put on the facing.

Place the ruler along the edge of the shoulder and draw a straight line with it.

Trim the main fabric and the canvas underneath to this line.

If there are any bits of the canvas showing around the edge of the armhole, trim those as well.

Do not trim the lining yet.

Mark in the back shoulder seam in the same way and trim off.

Trim the lining around the armhole edge, back neck edge and shoulder seams, leaving about 1.3cm (½in) extra. This is again a safety measure, for making up the armholes later on.

Now join the shoulder seams, making sure you keep the lining, facing and canvasses out of the way and only join the fabric seams.

If your jacket has princess-line seams, make sure the seams match in the middle of the shoulder.

You will find that there is a little bit of ease in the shoulder at the back.

Press the shoulder seams open.

Setting the plastron

You now need to set the plastron in place. Lay the shoulder over your hand, along the shoulder seam. Make sure the canvas and shoulder seam are flat inside. Now place a pin just in front of the seam at both ends of the plastron.

Turn the seam over, lift the shoulder seam at the back of the jacket, taking the canvas as well. Stitch the canvas in place along the back seam as close to the seamline as possible.

Baste the rest of the canvas around the armhole, keeping the lining out of the way.

Now, for the first time since you started making up the whole garment, it looks as if it could actually be a jacket. I bet you won't be able to resist trying it on at this point!

Chapter 8

The Collar

My students usually say that they have problems with either the collar or the sleeves. I think that's probably because they are the two things which you see the most on a jacket. When you are talking to someone, you look at their face. The collar frames the face and so becomes more visible than the rest of the jacket, and the sleeves are an extension of this area. You have already started on this frame by making the lapel; that's all sitting perfectly, so let's get started on the rest of the collar.

On a man's jacket a very stiff collar canvas is used and applied in the same way as you are now going to do. I find this canvas too stiff for a woman's jacket, so I use duck linen for the job.

The Under Collar

The under collar is always cut on the crosswise direction of both the fabric and the duck linen canvas which is used as an interlining. This is so the collar can be shaped into a curve to fit around the neckline of the jacket. Pad stitching will be used on the under collar to achieve this shaping, in a manner similar to the lapel, plus steam to get the correct shape.

The side edges of the collar are known as the fall, as this is the part of the collar which falls around the shoulders before you get into the stand area, which stands up around the back neckline.

1. Cutting the duck linen
Cut out the under collar shape in the duck linen canvas; this needs to be on the cross grain just as for the fabric collar. Remove the seam allowance along the centre back seam: duck linen, just like the canvas for the T-zone, doesn't like being pressed open.

2. Joining the centre back seam
This seam is stitched in the same way as the princess-line seam on the T-zone. It is a bit easier to stitch this one as it is a straight line, not shaped as before.

Take a strip of silk organza or lining about 3.8cm (1½in) wide and slightly longer than the centre back seam.

Place one side of the under collar to the middle of the organza strip and machine the under collar to the strip, stitching as close to the edge as you can.

Butt the other side of the collar to the first side and stitch again as for the first side. Then stitch both again about 6mm (¼in) away from the join.

Change the machine to a zigzag stitch and position the collar so that the zigzag stitch goes over the join.

Zigzag along the join, then trim off any excess organza from the back of the collar.

3. Stitching the break line
Now place the duck linen canvas on top of the wrong side of the under collar. Stitch the two layers of the collar together along the break line.

This is the line along the collar where it folds over around the back of the neck. It will form a continuous line which matches up to the break line on the front of the jacket along the lapel.

Start and finish machining this stitching line 2cm (¾in) from the edge of the collar. If the break line is not marked on the pattern, there are a couple of ways of getting the position marked for it. The first, and probably the most accurate, is to baste the collar onto the jacket and try it on. When you fold back the collar into its finished position you will see exactly where it needs to be for your personal fitting.

Another way of doing it is to fold the

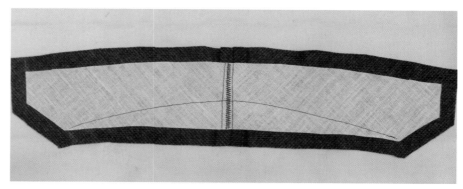

Stitching the break line.

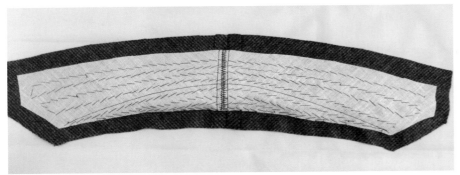

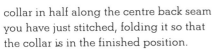

Pad stitching the under collar.

Turning in the edges of the collar.

collar in half along the centre back seam you have just stitched, folding it so that the collar is in the finished position.

Using tailor's chalk, put a mark on the seamline 6mm (¼in) below the fold. This allows the collar to fold back and cover the seam holding the collar in place when the jacket is finished. This stitching line will not be seen once the collar is complete.

The two ends of this line are at the notch on the collar on the edge where it joins the jacket. Join all three of these points up in a slow gentle curve. Machine a line of stitching along this line, attaching the two layers together.

Carefully mark and trim off 2cm (¾in) all round the edge of the duck linen. This removes all of the seam allowance, plus 2mm (⅛in) to allow for the canvas moving when rolling the collar whilst pad stitching. Make sure, when you have trimmed the canvas, that both sides of the collar are exactly the same shape and size.

4. Pad stitching the under collar
You now need to pad stitch the two layers together. This is done in exactly the same way as the lapel.

Work the stitches from the machined roll line out across the stand area towards the neck edge, using stitches about 1cm (⅜in) long. Follow the shape of the canvas out to the edge, rolling the collar as you go. Stop stitching when you get to the edge of the canvas.

When you have covered the stand area, turn the collar round and pad stitch from the break line out towards the back edge of the collar, using the same size of stitches as for the stand.

If you look at the shape of the area you are stitching, you will find that the centre back part of the collar is narrower than the sides of the collar.

Instead of doing small spaced rows of stitching all the way across the collar, you will need to do the small spaced rows at the centre back, but when you get to the ends of the collar, fan the rows of stitching out slightly wider at the edges.

This makes it easier, as you don't have to do lots of short rows of pad stitching.

You need to roll this part of the collar as well. Stop the stitching 1cm (⅜in) away from the edge of the duck linen.

When you have finished the stitching, the collar will look like a sausage all curled up. Don't panic; this is exactly what you need.

5. Checking the collar shape
Now check that both sides of the duck linen are exactly the same shape and size by laying one side of the collar on top of the other side.

Trim if necessary; the whole of the seam allowance should be removed from the duck linen all the way around the collar.

You only need to trim this off if the pad stitching has skewed the edges.

At the top and bottom of the centre back seam, trim the seam allowance on the main fabric at an angle to make it less bulky.

6. Turning in the edges of the collar
Leave the bottom edge with a full amount of seam allowance.

Tuck the seam allowance along the sides and top edge of the collar behind the duck linen.

Fold the seam in, so that you can see only 3mm (⅛in) of the duck linen above the fold line.

Baste this turning into place. When you are basting, don't stitch on the outside edge of the fold, as you are going to tuck the top collar in between this folded edge and around the duck linen.

Make sure the basting is about 6mm (¼in) in from the edge.

Fasten the two ends of the collar first

Bottom edge of the under collar.

and then go across the top edge.

7. Bottom edge of the under collar

Using the duck linen as your template, baste the seam allowance of the collar over the duck linen along the bottom edge of the collar.

Then herringbone stitch this seam down to the duck linen.

Remove the basting stitches holding the seam in place; it's easier to do this now whilst the collar is still flat.

Basting the under collar into place.

Fastening the bridle.

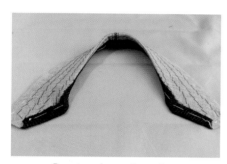

Pressing the under collar.

8. Pressing the under collar

The under collar needs to be pressed at this point.

First press round all the edges, making sure that the seam allowance is tucked in and secure. Then press in the break line, following the shape carefully.

9. Shaping the back edge of the collar

If you look at the top edge of the collar it looks very straight compared to where it will be worn (that is, the rounded shape of your neck) so you need to stretch the collar into shape.

To do this place the left-hand side of the collar flat on the ironing board.

The end of the collar needs to stay flat, so starting about 7.5cm (3in) in from the side of the collar, put some steam into the collar and pull and stretch the collar round to form the shape of the neckline.

It won't need too much stretching, as it is cut on the bias grain.

Once you have done the left side, place the right-hand side of the collar flat on the ironing board and repeat the stretching, this time starting with the stretching from the centre back and working out towards the edge of the collar. Stop stretching the collar about 7.5cm (3in) from the side of the collar.

10. Basting the under collar into place

Place the under collar onto the neckline of the jacket. The finished edge of the under collar will sit on the 1.5cm (⅝in) seamline.

If you find it easier to see the seam allowance, mark it in using tailor's chalk; you can then place the edge of the collar to the line.

The straight, front edge of the bottom of the under collar should be placed so that its edge is level with the magic dot at the front. When you get to the other end of the straight edge it should be on the top edge of the break line. Pin the collar in place.

From the break line around to the centre back seam, the collar should be placed on to the seamline. It should sit very easily into position.

Repeat the two steps above to get the other half of the collar into place. Then baste this part of the collar into place using large sideways basting stitches.

To form these sideways stitches, make a small running stitch at right angles to the collar edge, then move along the

edge of the collar by 1.5cm (⅝in) and make another running stitch.

The effect of this stitch is similar to the edge basting along the lapel and front edge.

Note: Using this form of basting makes a more secure basting line to keep the collar in place whilst you position the top collar.

The basting stitches should be on the edge of the bottom of the under collar.

Fold the collar into its finished position, just to check that everything is sitting correctly.

11. Fastening the bridle

Turn the jacket to the wrong side. You should be able to see where you finished pad stitching the bridle when you made up the lapel.

Lay the loose end of the bridle down so that the middle of it continues along the break line onto the under collar.

Trim the bridle off if it extends beyond the shoulder seam.

Pad stitch this part of the bridle into place, starting where you left off from the lapel. The stitches should be the same size and width apart as the lapel stitching.

Doing this pad stitching will extend the support of the bridle into the collar, stopping the break line from stretching out.

The Top Collar

1. Shaping the collar

You need to shape the top collar in a way similar to the under collar. The steaming process is the same except that you need to shrink the bottom edge of the collar as you go. This stretching and shrinking process will seem a bit harder than for the under collar: this is because the under collar is cut on the cross grain whereas the top collar is on the straight grain.

Shaping the top collar.

To shape the top collar, lay the fabric on the ironing board. Leave the first 12.5cm (5in) flat on the board. Pull the top edge of the collar and put plenty of steam into the section of the collar from 12.5cm (5in) in from the edge to the centre back of the collar.

As you pull it into shape you will see small waves appearing at the bottom edge; if you put lots of steam into this part of the collar you can shrink away these waves. Only use a little bit of

Finishing the edge of the facing.

pressure on this edge. If you try to press it flat by using the weight of the iron, you will just press pleats into the bottom edge.

Repeat this technique from the centre back out to 12.5cm (5in) from the front edge.

Leave the top collar to one side to let it dry and set completely before putting it onto your jacket.

2. Finishing the edge of the facing

Before putting the top collar on the jacket, you need to finish off the edge of the facing. Start at the magic dot and finish at the shoulder seam.

Turn in the seam allowance along the edge of the facing, neatly turning the edge so that, at the magic dot, the fold looks as if it is a continuation of the top of the lapel.

When you get to the corner of the facing you will have to snip into the seam allowance to enable you to turn the rest of the seam allowance under.

The folded edge should run in exactly the same line as the under collar edge underneath.

Basting the top collar into place.

3. Basting the top collar into place

Once the collar has been shaped, you need to lay it over the top of the duck linen interfacing, positioning the top collar so that there is plenty of fabric overlapping all the edges.

Remember how, when you cut out the collar, you didn't cut it to the shape of the pattern; you just cut an oblong of

fabric, bigger than the pattern. This is to allow for ease.

Sew a row of large basting stitches across the back edge of the collar, about 2.5cm (1in) in from the back edge of the collar. As you baste, ease a small amount of fabric into the collar sideways.

Turn the top collar into its finished position and then sew another row of basting stitches about 3.8cm (1½in) from the first one (a total of 6.3cm/2½in in from the back edge of the collar).

These two rows of basting will hold the collar in place whilst you turn in all the edges.

Turning in the edges of the collar.

4. Turning in the edges

The first edge to turn in is the one at the bottom of the collar where the collar meets the facing.

This is the edge which sits around the back of your neck, covering the stand area of the collar.

At both sides of this edge you will see that the top collar overlaps the finished edge of the facing; this extends right up to the shoulder seam.

Trim the seam allowance of the top collar down to 1cm (⅜in) from the shoulder seam.

Now tuck the seam allowance inside, so that the edge of the top collar butts up to the edge of the facing.

Follow the shape of the facing, folding the corner of the collar in when you get to the corner of the facing.

Turning in the top edge of the collar.

As you turn in this edge, keep checking that you are not pulling the collar tight or leaving too much excess fabric across the collar.

When you get to the shoulder seam, snip the seam of the top collar so that you can lay it flat.

In between the two shoulder seams the top collar is just basted flat. Do not turn in the edge of the fabric as it will make the collar too bulky if you turn this seam allowance in.

The lining will cover the raw edge of the fabric when it is finished. Baste the seam allowance into place, trimming where necessary to make it lay flat.

5. Turning in the top edge

Now go to the top edge of the collar. The seam allowance needs to be trimmed down to 1cm (⅜in). Bring the seam

allowance over the edge of the duck linen and tuck it in between the duck linen and the under collar. Use the duck linen as your template. Don't baste beyond 1cm (⅜in) at each end of the collar.

6. Turning in the ends of the collar

The last step in the collar preparation is to turn in the ends of the top collar. As you did with the top edge of the collar, trim down the excess seam allowance, leaving a 1cm (⅜in) seam.

Tuck this seam allowance round the duck linen and in between it and the under collar.

If the fabric seems a little bit too thick at the top and bottom of this edge, trim the seam allowance down diagonally. Check carefully before you trim.

7. Hand-finishing the collar

Finally, you need to hand-finish the collar. Turn the collar over, so that you are looking at the under collar; the edge of the collar needs to be slip stitched into place all the way round. The stitches need to be small and neat. Don't forget these stitches are all that is holding the collar in place; there is no machine stitching on this collar.

8. Drawing the collar

Turn your attention to the bottom edge of the collar where the two folded edges

butt together. You are going to sew these two edges together: this process is called drawing the collar and it starts at the right-hand side of the collar at the magic dot.

Use your ordinary sewing thread and put a knot at the end. Bring the needle up from under the folded edge of the top collar. Make sure you are right on the folded edge.

Now take a stitch from the fold on the facing, pick up a thread from the under collar which is lying beneath the two folds and then a small amount of cloth from the folded edge of the top collar. As you pull this stitch through you will see the two folded edges draw together, hence the name of the process. (This saves having to go inside the collar afterwards to do another row of stitching.)

Repeat this stitch until you get to the shoulder seam on the right-hand side of the collar.

Starting where you snipped into the collar at the shoulder seam, sew a row of small running stitches from one snip to the other, in between the two shoulder seams.

You are catching the top collar to the seam allowance of the neckline of the jacket.

Once you get to the shoulder seam on the left-hand side of the jacket, start to draw the rest of the seam together as before, finishing at the magic dot on the left-hand side of the collar.

Press the top collar to make sure everything is sitting smoothly before you move on.

Turning in the ends of the collar.

Drawing the collar.

Chapter 9

The Sleeves

Sleeves can be one of the trickiest parts of the jacket to get right. Anyone who tells you that they never have any trouble with sleeves is fibbing. On certain fabrics putting a sleeve in can be a problem. If you have invested in really good woollen cloth as shown here it should be fairly straightforward as the fabric moulds easily into shape.

Don't think that you have failed with the sleeve if you have to undo a bit and resew it; I have unpicked many sleeves. Think of it as good practice for unpicking; the more you do it the better and faster you get at it!

If you follow the steps I'm about to show you, it should make putting a sleeve in much easier.

Making Up the Bottom of the Sleeve

You may remember when you did the first batch of stitching a while ago that you stitched the short seam (forearm seam) and pressed it open, so you can now lay the sleeve flat on the table, right side uppermost.

1. Marking in the hemline

You are going to mark up the bottom of the sleeve first, using a sharp piece of tailor's chalk and a ruler. Using the tailor tacks as a guide, mark in the hemline on the front of the upper sleeve only. Remove the tailor tacks along the hemline.

2. Strengthening the vent

You need to fuse a piece of fusible interfacing to the wrong side of the sleeve along the hemline to give it some support.

Cut a piece of Washable Supersoft interfacing the width of the sleeve and about 10cm (4in) wide.

Cut this piece with the straight grain of the fabric going down the 10cm (4in) width.

Along the top edge of this piece cut a slow gentle curve in the middle.

Don't leave it straight or you will be able to see a shadow along the top edge through from the right side when you are wearing the jacket.

Fuse the interfacing into place, positioning it so that you have 2.5cm (1in) of the interfacing below the hemline and the rest of it above.

3. Marking in the vent and buttons

Now mark in the 1.5cm (⅝in) seam allowance just above the top of the extra fabric allowed for the vent.

Using the ruler and tailor's chalk,

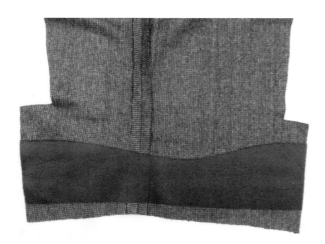

Strengthening the vent.

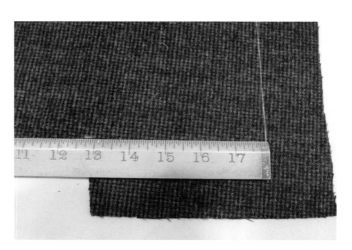

Marking in the vent.

mark a line down from the top of the vent to the hemline. Make sure that your ruler forms a right angle with the hemline.

If you don't have the right angle now, when you make up the sleeve it won't sit level around the bottom cuff edge when the sleeve is finished.

Decide how many buttons you want on your cuff. Use the following measurements for marking up from the hemline of the sleeve.
1. button: 4.5cm (1¾in)
2. buttons: 7cm (2¾in)
3. buttons: 9.5cm (3¾in)

These measurements allow for a button which is 1.5cm (⅝in) in diameter. If you have larger or smaller buttons you will have to adjust the length of the vent.

Mark a line in chalk for the length of the opening you have decided on.

4. Marking in the rest of the sleeve
Fold the sleeve over as if you were about to stitch the long seam (hindarm) on the sleeve.

Carefully lay the front of the sleeve onto the under sleeve and measure the seam down to the bottom, making sure everything fits together. Once you are happy with the way the sleeve sits, bang

along the hemline transferring some of the chalk through to the under sleeve. The chalk lines will be faint so, if necessary, draw in the lines to reinstate the chalk.

Be sure that you lay the sleeve with the upper sleeve on top or the chalk won't show through. You can't defy gravity!

Open the sleeve out again and re-mark the hemline all the way across the bottom of the sleeve, joining up the first line you drew in to the banged-through chalk on the under sleeve.

You will see that there is a faint line down the side of the sleeve; this is where

Marking in the rest of the sleeve.

Removing excess fabric from the vent.

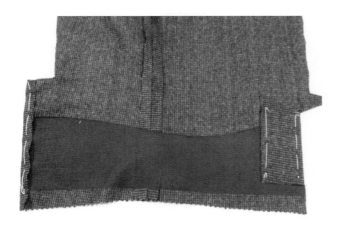
Basting up the vent.

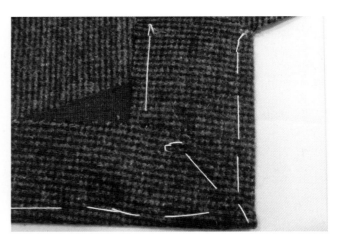
Basting the hemline and creating a mitred corner.

the chalk mark is for the vent on the other side. Place your ruler against this line towards the edge of the sleeve and then draw another chalk line on the opposite side of the ruler. You will find that there is a bit of fabric left after that towards the edge of the sleeve. This will be your seam allowance for the under part of the vent finish.

I recommend finishing the bottom of the hemline off by using a pair of pinking shears, just as you did on the bottom hemline on the jacket.

5. Removing excess fabric from the vent
There are two places where you need to trim the fabric around the vent. The first one is to snip diagonally into the top of the vent right into the place where you want the vent to start.

Make sure you snip right to the line or you won't be able to make the vent up properly.

The second place is at the bottom of the vent on the front of the sleeve. You need to remove some of the excess fabric to enable you to make a neat finish to the inside of the sleeve.

Coming up from the bottom of the sleeve, snip along a line which is in line with the side of the vent until you get to around 1cm (³⁄₈in) from the hemline.

Then go to the side of the vent and snip along 1cm (³⁄₈in) below the hemline until you reach the first snip so that you can then remove a small square of fabric.

6. Basting up the vent
Turn in the side edges of the vent and, using basting thread, baste these turnings into place; the stitches need to be about 1cm (³⁄₈in) from the edge.

On the upper sleeve this will be all the extra fabric allowed for the vent, from the snip to the hemline. This side will need another row of basting to hold the inside edge down.

On the lower sleeve just turn in the seam allowance.

7. Basting the sleeve hemline
Turn up the hemline and baste it into place. On the side of the sleeve which has the underside of the vent (the under sleeve) you can just baste this flat; it will

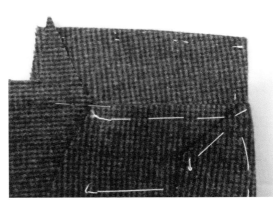
Sleeve seam.

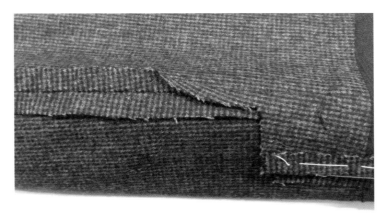
Pressing the vent in place.

Basting the vent in place.

Lining in the sleeve.

sit neatly for you.

On the side which has the vent on it (the top sleeve) you need to create a mitred corner. Just fold the edge of the sleeve at 45 degrees to the hemline and fold in. Once you have created this angle you will be able to baste it flat.

8. Finishing the bottom of the sleeve

Hand-stitch the edges and hem of the sleeve by folding back the edge of the seam allowance fabric by 6mm (¼in), then slip stitching it into place. Once you let the hemline sit flat again it will cover up your stitching.

This technique is exactly the same as you did when fastening the hem of the jacket. Then slip stitch the two folded sides of the vent from top to bottom.

Next, you need to press the bottom of the sleeve and the vent.

This is the last chance you will have to give the bottom of the sleeve a good press as you will be stitching the second seam next; this is the last time you will be able to lay the sleeve flat.

If the basting thread marks your fabric when it is pressed, you will need to remove the basting stitches before you press. Make sure you use plenty of steam and then the point presser afterwards to get a really sharp edge to your sleeve.

The sleeve seam

1. Stitching the long seam (hindarm)

Before you stitch, lay the seam together so that you can see the finished vent on top. Check that the hemlines at the bottom are level. Put a pin into the bottom of the seam exactly where the seam starts. Pin the rest of the seam together and stitch a 1.5cm (⅝in) seam. You need to be exactly on the snip at the bottom of the sleeve.

Note: A mistake my students often make when stitching this seam is to not quite catch the snip right into the seam.

2. Pressing and basting the vent in place

Press the seam open as before. You will only be able to press as far as the start of the vent.

Lay the mitred side of the vent flat, then lay the underside of the vent on top of it.

Let the seam sit as it naturally lies, then press in place. Don't try to force it into position or snip it (as you will weaken the sleeve if you snip in).

Turn the sleeve to the right side and give the seam a good press from this side.

Baste the vent in place at the bottom of the sleeve.

Turn the sleeve back to the wrong side.

1. Short seams

Locate the sleeve lining which had the two seams stitched in the first phase of sewing.

Lay the lining on top of the sleeve, starting with the short seams together. You allowed an extra 1.3cm (½in) in the armhole of the lining, so place this extra above the sleeve.

Baste the two short seams together from top to bottom. Start the row of basting 6.3cm (2½in) from the top of the sleeve; this will give you some room to keep the lining out of the way whilst you put the sleeve into the armhole.

As you stitch this row of basting, ease a small amount to the lining into the seam, just to ensure the lining isn't pulling tight. You will only be able to stitch to the hemline of the seam.

You will be basting through one side of the sleeve seam and the two sides of the lining, as you didn't press the lining seams open. Baste as close to the seams as possible. Note that, although you are just basting these seams, these rows of stitching will stay inside the jacket.

2. Basting the second seam lining

Now turn the sleeve over and stitch the long seams together, again placing the lining 1.3cm (½in) above the main fabric of the sleeve. Start basting the seams together as before but start the stitching level with the start of the basting on the short seam.

Baste down the sleeve as far as you can go, keeping the seam flat.

3. Basting the lining to the bottom of the sleeve

You now need to turn the sleeve so that the lining is in its finished position. To do this quickly and easily, put your arm down the lining sleeve, catch hold of the fabric sleeve at the bottom and pull the whole thing through.

Hey presto! The lining is in position.

Now trim the lining so it is 1.3cm (½in) below the finished edge of the

Basting the second seam lining.

sleeve. Be careful not to trim the bottom of the sleeve at the same time!

Now turn the lining in so it finishes 2.5cm (1in) above the bottom of the sleeve and baste it in place. This row of basting stitches needs to be on the edge of the lining.

Because you have the two rows of stitching down the seams, this should stop the lining being pulled tight at the bottom, but just check before you baste the edge in place that the lining still sits perfectly flat.

Turn the sleeve through to the right side.

Basting the lining to the bottom of the sleeve.

Preparing the Sleeve for Placement

Keeping the lining out of the way, machine a row of easing stitches around the crown of the sleeve using the sewing machine.

The stitching needs to start just below the long seam (hindarm) and go over the crown (top edge) of the sleeve to a position on the front sleeve level with the start of the stitching.

Machine from the right side of the sleeve with the stitch length set at the longest your machine will do.

Don't fasten off the ends of this row of stitching; leave them long enough to grip for the easing process later.

The row of stitching needs to be 3mm (⅛in) wider than the seam allowance, which means you will be stitching on the finished part of the sleeve.

This may seem like a strange place to be stitching but if you draw up this row of basting you will find that just beyond it there is a flat area before the wavy edge of the seam allowance kicks in. This is where you will be stitching the sleeve into the armhole.

I like to pull the basting row up a little to start the shaping of the crown of the sleeve. Pull the stitches up from the wrong side from both ends.

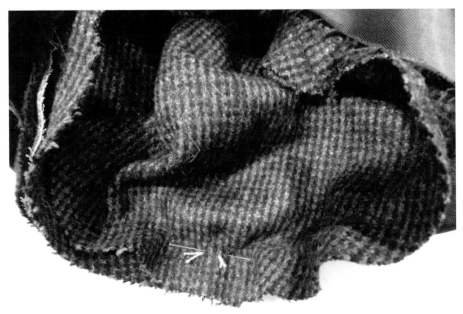

Positioning the sleeve.

If you turn the sleeve over to the right side, you will see the finished rounded top of the sleeve start to appear before you.

I usually start with the left sleeve. I don't know the reason why, but this sleeve always seems to go in a little easier than the right one. Whichever sleeve you are doing, the positioning of it is the same.

Keep the lining from the body and the sleeves out of the way whilst you are doing all of the next few steps. You will deal with the lining separately once the sleeve is safely in the correct position.

1. Positioning the sleeve

First, match the tailor tack which is on the underarm or side seam of the jacket to the tailor tack on the under sleeve. Put a pin in to keep the sleeve in place.

Go to the top of the sleeve and match the tailor tack in the sleeve to the shoulder seam. Pin the sleeve into place at this point. When you are pinning you should pin from the sleeve side; you will be working inside the sleeve.

As a quick check on the sleeve, turn the sleeve to the right side and hang the sleeve from your hand. By doing this you can check to see if the sleeve is hanging correctly. If it's in the right place the sleeve should point slightly towards the front of the jacket, as if your arm were inside. By doing this check you can also tell if you have the correct sleeve in the armhole. I have, on a number of occasions, seen people go through all the following stages to get the sleeve right, only to discover they have put the sleeve into the wrong armhole.

Now you have the sleeve secured at the top and bottom you can start to see what needs to be done to get this sleeve into position. Most of the ease in the sleeve needs to be within about 10cm (4in) on either side of the shoulder position.

You are going to start at the pin at the bottom of the armhole on the underarm;

either side of this pin is where the sleeve needs the least ease. That's not to say that you don't need any ease at all; just pin the sleeve into position easing a little fabric into the sleeve as you go. Position the pins so they form a mock stitching line. Keep pinning until you get to the basting stitches.

The sleeve seams and the seams around the jacket body are not cut to match.

Have a look at the amount of ease you have in the head of the sleeve; this is the amount that you need to accommodate.

Pull the easing up so that the sleeve fits into the armhole.

2. Easing the crown of the sleeve

To make it easier to see where the fullness needs to go, put your fingertips underneath the body of the jacket, pushing the sleeve onto the top.

This will put the fullness in reverse of where it will be once the sleeve is machined in, but it is easier to see where to put the fullness without turning the

sleeve through to the right side every time you alter it.

Move the fullness so you don't have any tucks in the sleeve head. Pin into place as before. Keep checking the edges of the sleeve and armhole are level. You are looking for a nice rounded shape to the top of the sleeve with no pleats or bumps in it.

When you are happy with the sleeve, turn it to the right side and hang the jacket from your fingertips.

You should be able to see how the sleeve looks.

Check for any hollows or pleats. If you spot anything that doesn't look quite right, move the fullness up or down the sleeve.

Don't let the edge of the sleeve creep out over the edge of the jacket; the shape of the sleeve will mean that the sleeve will naturally want to do this and you need to control it.

If it takes control, you will finish up with a flat crown to the top of your

Easing the crown of the sleeve.

sleeve.

It is worth spending a bit of time at this stage getting the sleeve sitting perfectly.

When you are completely happy with the positioning of the sleeve, turn once again to the wrong side of the sleeve. Cut a piece of organza selvedge to 1.3cm (½in) in width; this piece needs to be slightly longer than the distance around the sleeve.

You could also use a 6mm (¼in) cotton stay tape for doing this job but make sure it is very well shrunk before putting it into your sleeve. You will be using a lot of steam on this sleeve head and you don't want the stay tape to shrink as you are doing it.

3. Positioning the stay tape

Starting at the underarm seam, pin this strip into place, matching the raw edge of the selvedge to the edge of the seam allowance. The pins will only be going through the tape and sleeve seam, *not* through to the armhole of the jacket.

When you get to the fullness in the head of the sleeve, place the tape down so it squashes the fullness out of the way; the tape will be exactly the same size as the armhole.

Be careful to squash the fullness down where you placed it when positioning

the sleeve. Don't let the fullness escape further along the seam. If this happens you will finish up with lots of ease at the top of the sleeve and it will most likely form pleats.

When you get all the way around the armhole, overlap the tape by 1.3cm (½in).

Once the tape is in place, carefully remove the positioning pins placed into the seam, so that you are able to lift the sleeve out of the armhole with the organza stay tape in place.

The shape of the sleeve will remain the same as the armhole of the jacket.

4. Stitching the tape

Using a single thread, hand-stitch the tape in place using a small running stitch. About every three or four stitches do a backstitch; this will secure the tape and stop it from moving around the sleeve.

This row of stitches will be just inside the edge of the selvedge. Remove the pins as you stitch.

When you have gone all round the sleeve, you should be able to see the shape of the finished sleeve.

5. Shrinking out the fullness

Now take the sleeve to the iron. Turn the sleeve so that you have the top, where most of the fullness is, on the ironing

board.

Using plenty of steam, shrink the fullness away, using the same technique as you did when shrinking out the bottom of the shaping on the top collar. You will only be able to do a small amount of the sleeve at a time.

Work your way all round the edge of the sleeve.

Pin the sleeve back into the armhole, pinning from the sleeve side. Start by matching the underarm and shoulder seams, just as you did when positioning the sleeve into the armhole.

Then pin in between these two positions. With the shaping permanently stitched in place, this should be just like pinning two straight edges together.

Make sure you keep the linings of both the sleeve and the jacket out of the way. The canvas around the front edge of the armhole should be pinned in with the sleeve.

Machine the sleeve into place, using a 1.5cm (⅝in) seam allowance. You should be stitching just outside the edge of the stay tape. There will be no ease to deal with as you stitch.

Then, with the sleeve in place, machine another short row of stitching, 6mm (¼in) inside the first one, starting and finishing 7.5cm (3in) either side of

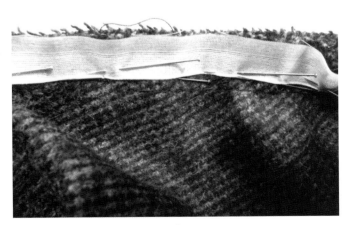

Positioning the stay tape.

Stitching the stay tape.

Shrinking out the fullness.

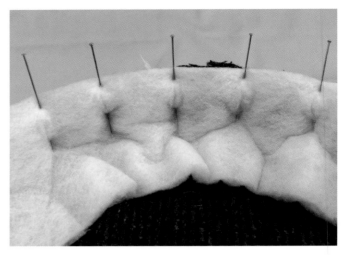
Positioning the volume fleece.

the underarm seam.

This is a strengthening row, so that when you are wearing your jacket and stretch forward it doesn't put too much strain on the first row of stitching.

Remove the row of ease stitching you put in when you first started making up the head of the sleeve. If you remove this row from the wrong side of the sleeve it should come out easily.

Trim the seam allowance all round the armhole down to 1cm (⅜in). Don't trim any further than this because you need some seam allowance on which to sit the pad.

Trimming the seam allowance down can be quite tricky, as you need to remove fabric from the armhole of the jacket, the sleeve seam and the edge of the plastron at the front of the sleeve. If the assembled layers are too thick for the shears to go through in one cut, cut through each layer separately.

Turn the jacket through to the right side and admire the beautiful sleeve you have just put in. It looks fantastic but it will look even better with the next stage of the process.

You are going to pad out the gap where the fullness of the sleeve and the jacket meet.

The fullness you have just stitched into the top of the sleeve can collapse when you are wearing it. There are quite a few ways of padding this space to prevent this happening; lots of tailors use sleeve heads stitched onto the inside of the sleeve.

Sleeve heads can be made of quite a few different things (canvas, felt, etc.) and can vary in size.

I don't like sleeve heads in my jackets as I find them a bit too bulky for me, so I make a sleeve wrap instead. You could use both a sleeve head and a sleeve wrap if you wanted to have a very padded sleeve crown.

6. The sleeve wrap
Cut a piece of volume fleece about 20cm (8in) long x 6cm (2⅜in) wide. You could cut this strip longer if you wanted more padding along the edge of the sleeve. It could even extend down as far as 7.5cm (3in) above the underarm seam. The easiest way is to try it out and see what length you prefer. You will be cutting the width of this strip down after it is in place, but it is easier to work with it a bit wider than you need.

7. Positioning the volume fleece
Fold this piece in half and place the centre point to the shoulder seam. Pin it in place, working from the sleeve side. When you place the pins, put them in at right angles to the seam, with the head of the pin on the outside of the seam. This is totally opposite to the way I've been telling you to pin all the way through this book. There is a reason: you are going to machine the volume fleece into place from the jacket side of the armhole, so that you can see the seamline you have just attached the sleeve with. If you position the pins like this, you will be able to remove them easily as you stitch.

Continue to pin the volume fleece in place from the shoulder seam to both ends.

Turn the sleeve to the inside and then machine a row of stitching from the jacket side of the seam. You need to be stitching alongside the row of stitching holding the sleeve in place.

Position this row of stitches so that it is far enough away from the seam that you can get another row of stitching in between these two rows.

Don't make the mistake of stitching

Wrapping the seam.

too far away, as you need at least 6mm (¼in) of volume fleece to be able to form the wrap. The closer you can get to the seamline the better.

8. Wrapping the seam

Once this row of machining is in place, go to the inside of the sleeve again. Bring the volume fleece out of the sleeve and wrap it round the seam allowance. You need to bring it quite tightly around the seam. Pin it into place, putting the pins alongside the sleeve seamline.

Have a look down into the armhole and you will see that the volume fleece is holding the sleeve out, giving it a beautiful, padded look.

Machine the volume fleece into place, removing the pins as you go.

Trim off any excess volume fleece from around the armhole, cutting as close as you can get to the seam you have just sewn.

Turn your jacket to the right side and see your sleeve with its padding in place. You should be looking at a lovely, rounded sleeve crown which doesn't look as if it fell out of the 1980s!

The sleeve will look beautiful and there is no need to press a sleeve which has been put in correctly. If you start pressing it now, you will ruin the shape of the fullness. If you feel you need to press it, it's not in correctly!

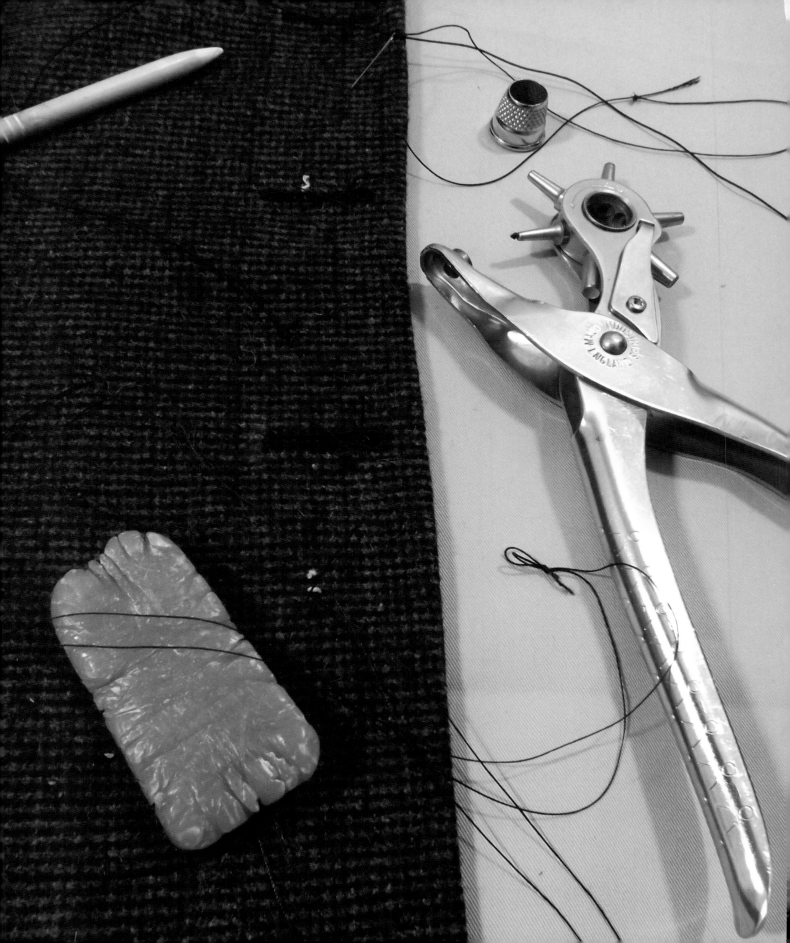

Chapter 10

Hand-Finishing

This is probably my favourite part of making a jacket. All the hard work is done, and you can relax and put the finishing touches to your jacket.

The full description of how to work all the stitches used in the finishing process can be found in Chapter 1 of this book.

Making Up the Armholes

To finish off the sleeves you need to put in the shoulder pads. I always use felt shoulder pads for this job: these are made of layers of felt stitched together. The felt doesn't change shape or squash when you are stitching them in place, so you will know exactly what size your pads are before you put them in and they will always remain that shape. You can cut down the layers of felt pads before you stitch them in if you feel they are too large for you. When you tried the jacket on at the fitting stage you made

allowances for the pads then; make sure you are using the same size of pad now.

1. Positioning the shoulder pad

Fold the shoulder pad in half; the halfway point of the pad is placed to the shoulder seam. When you do this the pad needs to be upside down to the way it will be when it is finished.

This looks very strange when you first do it but the pad will be turned over when you wear it. If you put the pad in so that it looked in its finished position, it would definitely look wrong when you were wearing it.

2. Stitching the shoulder pad

Place the pad to the shoulder so that the edge of the pad is level with the outside edge of the armhole seam.

Work your way along the pad to the end, dropping it back towards the seamline. When you get to the end of the pad, the edge should just be inside the seam allowance.

Backstitch the pad into place using a double basting thread. Work the stitches

as close as possible to the machining line holding the sleeve in place. The stitches need to be about 1.3cm (½in) long.

Don't be tempted to stitch on the edge of the seam allowance as the pad will just look as if it is falling away: you need the seam allowance as support to hold it in place.

As you get towards the shoulder seam bring the edge of the pad out towards the edge of the seam allowance.

Once you get to the middle of the pad (shoulder seam), continue to stitch as before but start to bring the pad back towards the stitching line. Stitch until you get to the end of the shoulder pad.

By dropping the pad back towards the seam at both ends, you create a little bit of ease in the pad. This will stop you getting puckers in the front of your jacket.

Turn the jacket to the right side and drape the shoulder pad over your hand.

Check to see that it's lying correctly.

Positioning the shoulder pad.

Stitching the shoulder pad.

Securing the edge of the shoulder pad.

The fabric around the pad should be nice and smooth with no fabric puckering up at either side.

Once you are happy put a pin into the shoulder seam at the opposite edge of the pad to where you have just backstitched it.

This pin will hold the edge of the pad in the correct position whilst you secure the rest of the shoulder pad in place.

3. Securing the edge of the shoulder pad

Turn the jacket back to the inside so that you can fasten the edge of the pad to the plastron at the front of the jacket.

Using a single thread of basting cotton, herringbone stitch over the edge of the pad to keep it in place.

The stitches need to be fairly large and not too tight. Make sure you are only stitching to the plastron and not going through to the jacket fabric.

The next step is to fasten the body lining around the armhole edges.

The basting you did when you lined the jacket in during the basting under process has left you with a gap of about 5cm (2in) between it and the sleeve seam. It should therefore be fairly easy to lay the lining around the armhole and baste it into position without pulling it tight or leaving it too loose.

4. Basting the lining round the armhole edge

Start with the left sleeve and lay the lining flat. Starting at the shoulder seam on the front panel and using a single

thread of basting cotton, baste the lining in place.

You will be basting clockwise around the armhole.

Your stitching line should be just inside the seam allowance you used to stitch the sleeve into place. As you baste you will be able to feel the seam allowance through the lining, giving you a guide as to where you should place your basting.

Continue stitching until you get to about 5cm (2in) before the shoulder seam on the back panel. Fold in the seam allowance on the shoulder seam at the back shoulder, and then baste over it.

You need to do the same thing on the right sleeve but there is a slight variation to doing it because it is impossible to baste anti-clockwise unless you are left-handed.

If you are left-handed you will face

this problem on the left sleeve.

So when you start to baste this armhole you will have to start on the back panel. Start about 5cm (2in) down from the shoulder seam and baste the lining in place as before. Once you have stitched around the armhole to the front panel, you can then go back and stitch the 5cm (2in) gap at the beginning, turning the seam inside along the shoulder seam of the back panel.

These rows of basting will be staying in the jacket even when it is finished.

Check that the lining is sitting perfectly in the correct position. If necessary, try the jacket on to check that the lining is sitting comfortably.

When you are happy with it, trim off the excess lining hanging over the armhole edge.

When both armholes have been basted into position you progress to the shoulder and back neck area.

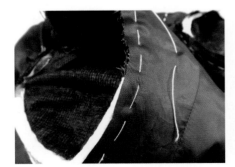

Basting the lining round the armhole edge.

Basting the back neck edge.

Finishing the Neck Edge and Sleeve Lining

1. Basting the back neck edge
You have already started the process of folding the lining in along the shoulder edges when you basted the lining round the armhole. Continue to fold this seam allowance underneath and baste into place until you reach the neck edge.

When you get to the neck edge, turn in the seam allowance along this edge as well. Keep the centre back pleat folded in place.

Fold the seam of the lining around the back neck. Neatly cover the raw edge of the top collar. You may need to trim the seam allowance down to make it sit properly.

With this all basted into place, all that is left is to fell stitch it in place.

Start at the shoulder edge on the left-hand sleeve, stitch up to the end of the shoulder, across the back neck and continue across the right-hand shoulder seam to the edge of the pad.

2. Stitching the sleeve lining in place
Bring the lining up out of the sleeve. Fold in the seam allowance and fell stitch it to the armhole just covering the row of basting stitches which hold the body lining in place.

To make this process easier, crease a fold line to follow as you are hand-stitching by turning the seam allowance to the wrong side of the lining and running your fingernail along to crease the line.

3. Positioning the sleeve lining in place
Start with the short seam of the sleeve and place a pin on the sleeve seam from the inside, coming up through to the armhole of the jacket. Make sure that the sleeve lining seam is tucked inside and that the row of basting stitches is covered. Position the seam on top of the pin. Remove this pin and replace it with a pin on the top of the sleeve lining.

Go to the long seam and repeat this process.

These two pins will anchor the sleeve lining in place. I prefer to only use these two pins and go ahead and hand-stitch the lining in place easing in any fullness as I go.

If you don't feel that confident about hand-stitching, place more pins into the sleeve lining.

4. Felling the sleeve lining in place
Use a felling stitch to secure the lining in place. Work clockwise round the sleeve, taking a piece first from the armhole of the jacket and then from the sleeve lining. By sewing this way, the fullness should ease itself in.

The final step in finishing off the sleeves is to fell the lining in place at the bottom of the sleeve; this is easier to do if you turn the sleeve inside out. You need to stitch this lining along the edge.

Hand-Finishing the Rest of the Jacket

1. The bottom of the facing
The bottom of the facing is the place on the jacket that I get the most questions about. If you are not careful with the finishing here it can look very bulky and unprofessional.

First, fell stitch the edge of the facing into place along the bottom.

You will now be at the raw edge of the facing. If there are bits fraying out along this edge, trim them off so that you have a nice clean edge to the facing.

Now herringbone stitch this small raw edge into place, going over the edge of the facing. This stitch will finish off the

Positioning the sleeve lining in place.

Felling the sleeve lining in place.

Finishing the bottom of the facing.

Felling the bottom edge of the lining.

facing neatly without having to turn in the raw edge and create a bulky finish to the bottom of your jacket.

On the sample I have been making, I have the edge of the piping cord at the bottom of the facing. To finish this off, simply turn the raw edge in at the bottom of the jacket and catch this with the felling going across the bottom of the facing. Do another row of herringbone stitching across the raw edges as you did on the edge of the facing.

2. Felling the bottom edge

You now fell stitch the bottom of the lining in place. You don't want the stitches to be seen so you need to stitch underneath the folded edge of the lining.

Place your needle into the top layer of lining, in the middle of the gap between the row of basting and the folded edge of the hem.

Pull back the top layer of the lining to reveal the underneath of the fold; this creates a line for you to stitch along.

Once you have stitched all the way across the lining, go back and fell the two ends down to finish it off.

3. Prick stitching the edge

The next step is to hand-stitch the edges.

I recommend using a prick stitch for this process. The stitch needs to be worked from the right side of the fabric, so you will need to do it in three stages.

You need a single thread of your ordinary stitching thread.

If you wanted to make a design feature of the stitching, you could use a top stitching thread: this thread is a bit heavier than normal thread and will make the stitching stand out more.

You can position this row of stitching in one of two places; the choice is yours. I prefer to stitch as close as I can get to the edge of the jacket, but you could do this line 6mm (¼in) in from the edge. This is known as a 'quarter-off' in the trade. Stitching further in makes it more noticeable.

Start the stitching at the break point on the left-hand side of the jacket. Prick stitch up the lapel and round to the magic dot.

Continue to prick stitch all round the outside edge of the collar to the magic dot on the other side and then down to the break point at the bottom of the right-hand lapel.

Go back to the break point on the left-hand side.

Turn the jacket round so that you can work down to the bottom of the jacket and finish stitching on the edge of the front facing.

The last stage is to go to the edge of the facing on the right-hand side of the jacket and stitch up to the break point at the bottom of the right-hand lapel.

If you stitch the edges carefully you shouldn't really be able to make out that there is a stitch on the edge; it should just look as if there is an indent or prick in the fabric, hence the name of the stitch.

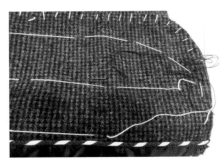

Fastening the facing to the canvas.

If you have a pocket with a flap on it or a welt pocket you will need to prick stitch these edges as well.

If you wanted to, you could prick stitch all the way down the seams too; again this would be a design feature.

4. Fastening the facing to the canvas

Another place that you need to use the prick stitch is on the inside of the facing, where you need to fasten the middle of the facing to the canvas underneath.

With a single thread, start stitching in the middle of the facing and work large prick stitches. This can be quite a tricky process as you don't want to let the stitches go through to the main fabric.

Work until you get to the shoulder, then start at the shoulder on the other side and continue to the bottom of the jacket.

Hand-Worked Buttonholes

The final stage of the finishing process is the hand-worked buttonholes.

Lots of my students get to this point

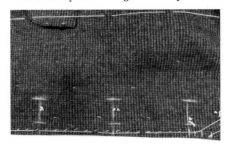

Marking the buttonholes.

and then have to talk themselves into punching a hole into their beautiful jackets. If you are not used to doing this type of buttonhole, I would do a few practice holes before going on to your jacket because a buttonhole worked clumsily can look like thick eyelashes covered in mascara sitting on the front of your jacket.

1. Marking the buttonholes

On a lady's jacket the buttonholes should be on the right-hand side of the jacket as viewed by the wearer.

When you did the fitting, you checked the position of the top and bottom buttonholes. If you are intending to use more than just the two buttons, you will need to mark the buttonhole positions between these two marks.

The extra buttons should be placed equal distances apart.

Use really sharp chalk to mark these lines.

Measure the diameter of your button. Divide this measurement in half: this is the distance that your buttonhole should start from the front edge of the jacket.

By measuring the half distance of the button in this way, it means that when you fasten up the jacket the buttons won't extend over the edge of the jacket front.

The length of the buttonhole should be the diameter of the button plus 3mm (⅛in); this amount will give room for the thickness of the button to pass through the buttonhole.

Double-check all these measurements before you cut the buttonhole. Once it's cut there is no going back.

2. Punching the keyhole

Now the scary bit. Using a hole punch on the smallest setting, go to the front of the buttonhole and punch your keyhole out.

This should be placed right on the cross where the middle of the buttonhole meets the front position.

Now take a pair of sharp scissors and carefully cut the buttonhole open to the chalk mark at the back of the buttonhole.

I have seen several methods of doing this process using chisels or quick unpicks. I find this method safer than most. If you are going to use a quick unpick, please put a pin across the end of your buttonhole to prevent you from cutting beyond the end of the buttonhole. You have spent a lot of time sewing this jacket; don't ruin it right at the end.

3. Securing the edges of the buttonhole

Turn the jacket to the wrong side. Using a single thread of ordinary cotton, oversew all round the edges of the buttonhole.

These stitches need to be small and close together.

If you just left the buttonhole with just this row of stitches in and nothing on top, it would function for quite a long time as a perfectly good buttonhole. However, the next steps make the buttonhole both durable and attractive.

Preparing the thread.

4. Preparing the thread for buttonhole stitching

You will need a single thread of either buttonhole twist or topstitching thread, depending on preference. Cut a one-metre length for each buttonhole and pull the lengths of thread through some beeswax.

Now take the thread to the iron and place onto a spare piece of cloth, fold the fabric over it and pull the thread through the heat of the iron. This will remove the excess wax and prevent it from getting onto your jacket.

Covering the thread will prevent any excess wax getting on either your iron or ironing board. Repeat for the other thread (or threads).

Make a knot in the end of each thread.

5. Fastening the thread at the starting position

On the right side, fasten the thread by putting the needle in about 1.3cm (½in) away from the buttonhole and bringing

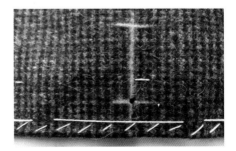

Punching the keyhole.

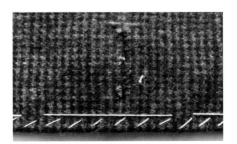

Securing the edges of the buttonhole.

Fastening the thread at the starting position.

Positioning the gimp.

Sewing the buttonhole stitch.

Trimming the gimp.

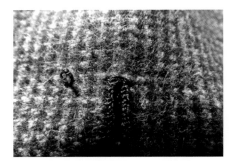

Making the bar tack.

the point out at the starting point for the buttonhole: this is at the end of the straight edge furthest away from the keyhole and about 3mm (⅛in) from the edge of the buttonhole.

The knot will be cut off after you have finished working the stitches for the buttonhole.

The work is done from the right side of the jacket and going clockwise round the buttonhole.

6. Positioning the gimp
Lay a length of gimp or a doubled topstitching thread along the edge of the buttonhole.

Leave about 1.5cm (⅝in) beyond the back edge of the buttonhole.

7. Sewing the buttonhole stitch
Place the needle under the edge of the buttonhole; the stitch width should be about 3mm (⅛in) wide.

Push the needle through until you have about 1.5cm (⅝in) of the point of the needle showing. Now wrap the thread clockwise around the needle.

Pull the needle through and tighten the thread to knot it into place.

The knots will form on the top edge of the buttonhole.

Work round the buttonhole, keeping the stitches close together. Follow the shape of the keyhole as you go. The stitches should be close together.

When you get to the end of the buttonhole, bring the thread to the wrong side of the fabric.

8. Trimming the gimp
Before making the bar tack, you need to trim off the ends of the gimp which are sticking out of the end of the buttonhole stitching.

Before you trim them off, gently pull on both ends of the gimp; this will make the buttonhole collapse a little in the middle.

Carefully trim the ends as close as you can get to the stitches but be careful not to cut the thread making the buttonhole.

Once the ends are trimmed, gently

Basting stitches on the buttonhole.

pull the buttonhole back to shape. This will send the ends of the gimp inside the buttonhole and you won't be able to see the untidy ends on the right side.

9. Making the bar tack
Bring the thread up so it is level with the outside of the last stitch worked. Now sew three or four long stitches from this point to the same point on the other side of the buttonhole where the outer point of your first stitch is.

The long stitches will be one on top of the other and form a base for your bar tack, just as the gimp has for the rest of the buttonhole.

Bring the thread up to level with the end of this row of stitching. Work four or five buttonhole stitches across the long stitches, going through the fabric as well as the stitches. This forms the bar tack.

Take the thread through to the wrong side of the jacket and work a couple of small backstitches to finish off.

Turn the jacket over and trim off the knot that you made when you started.

10. Basting threads on the buttonhole
Using the same thread, put a couple of large stitches across the buttonhole, forming a cross, and then a third one near the start of the keyhole. These will hold the buttonhole in place until you press them at the end of the sewing process.

11. Shaping the buttonhole
Using your two thumbnails, push the knots of the thread towards the edge of

Shaping the buttonhole.

the buttonhole: this will straighten the knots into the perfect position for pressing.

I like to put a bodkin into the keyhole and make sure that there is a satisfactory shape there too. If you don't have a bodkin a pencil will do the job just as well.

The buttonholes are the last part of the finishing process.

On a lady's jacket there are no buttonholes, real or sham, on the bottom of the cuff: the buttons are just stitched onto the top of the cuff.

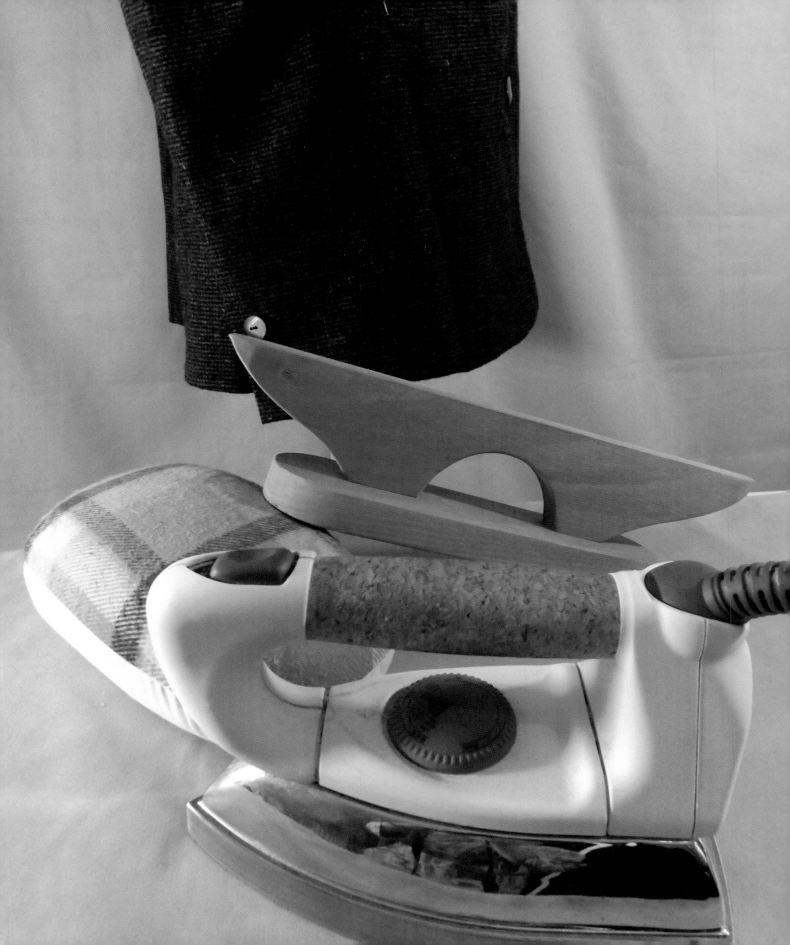

Chapter 11

Pressing Off and Final Touches

You now need to remove all the remaining basting stitches, except for the one holding the pleat in place along the lining on the centre back.

Leave the tailor tacks in both sides of the centre front and the ones marking the buttonholes on the left-hand side. Any other tailor tacks can now be removed.

To remove basting threads quickly and easily, go to the end of the basting thread where you did a backstitch to finish it off. Release this stitch and then go to the knot at the start of the length of thread. Pull this knot and the whole of the length should pull out. Sometimes the thread will break but this does not matter as it won't cut into the cloth of the jacket.

If you didn't take out the bastings when you made up the vents in the sleeves, this is usually where they hide, so check these.

Take a look at your jacket; this is when it really looks like a jacket.

If you have been folding or hanging the jacket up every time you leave it, there shouldn't be any deep creases in the jacket. However, you will need steam and heat to give it its final press.

Pressing the lining

I use a little steam on the lining. Start by pressing the lining flat all along the bottom edge. Make sure that the lining where you turned it back when stitching is lying flat. This should cover all the stitching inside the hemline.

Then work your way up the lining

Pressing the lining hem.

towards the armholes, smoothing out any creases as you go.

Make sure that the sleeves of the jacket are out of the way when doing this pressing. If you have pockets with flaps, they also need to be flat whilst you are pressing the lining of the jacket.

Gently press the pleat into the centre back; there is still a line of basting in this part of the jacket so only press lightly.

To press the armholes of the lining, turn the shoulders over so you can see the edges of the sleeve lining. Whilst balancing the sleeve on your fingers, carefully press around the armholes.

WARNING!

Be careful not to use steam for this part of the pressing: it will go straight through and burn your fingers underneath. Don't press too hard either; the iron is hot and it won't take long for the heat to hit your hand.

Pressing the armholes of the lining.

Lay the jacket down and press round the neck edge lining.

Pressing the right side of the jacket

If your fabric shines when you press it from the right side, cover it with a silk organza pressing cloth before you start the next pressing stages. You must keep on moving the cloth as you go.

Turn the jacket to the right side and start to press all the edges; put plenty of steam into the edges and then absorb it with the point presser. This will create a

Pressing the right side of the jacket.

beautifully sharp finish to the jacket.

Smooth out the rest of the jacket body; it shouldn't need a lot of pressing.

Whenever you get to a shaped part of the jacket, put it over the tailor's ham. You have worked extremely hard to put the shaping into the jacket so don't press it flat.

When you press over the front of the jacket where the pocket flap is, press and absorb the steam as before to create a sharp edge to the flap, then lift the flap up out of the way and press the jacket front flat again. Pressing over the flap would leave an imprint of the flap on the jacket front.

When you get to the right front you will be pressing over the buttonholes. This should make them look perfect, as the basting threads hold them securely in the perfect position.

To press the crease line into the collar, fold the collar back into its finished position, place it onto the tailor's ham to

Pressing the crease line into the collar.

form the shape of the neckline and press along the fold line.

Press the lining at the bottom of the sleeves very gently without using steam.

If there are any creases in the sleeve, hold the jacket up by putting your hand under the shoulder pad. Vertically steam the sleeve to make the creases drop out.

Do not try to lay the sleeve flat on the ironing board and press it: you will almost certainly press in creases that will

never come out.

Do not press the head of the sleeve. Leave the jacket hanging up, either on a dummy or a coat hanger, to dry out.

Buttoning the Jacket

1. Marking the position for the front buttons

Once the jacket has rested for a while to

Marking the position for the front buttons.

dry out you can mark in where the buttons need to be stitched. Lay the right front on top of the left front (as seen by the wearer), matching the centre front tailor tacks and the buttonholes to the tailor tacks.

Before you start marking through, double-check that everything is in the correct position.

Take a piece of tailor's chalk and, with

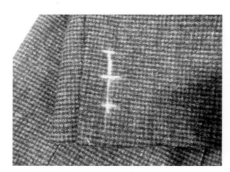

Marking the position for the cuff buttons.

your thumbnail, scrape some chalk through the keyhole of the buttonhole onto the left-hand side of the jacket below.

Remove the right front and mark with a cross the position of the buttons.

Now remove all the remaining tailor tacks from the fronts of the jacket.

2. Marking the position for the cuff buttons

You are now going to put in lines to mark the centres of the buttons. Using a ruler, draw a line 2cm (¾in) in from the vent edge. Measuring up from the bottom of the sleeve, mark for the first button 2.5cm (1in) up, and then draw a line every 2cm (¾in) above this line for as many buttons as you want on your cuff.

3. Sewing on the buttons

Use either buttonhole twist or topstitching thread for sewing the buttons on.

Use a double thread and pull it through the beeswax and the iron as you did when you made the buttonholes.

When sewing on the front buttons, you need to leave the threads coming through the button loose, so that you can make a shank below the button to strengthen it and make it sit above the buttonhole when it's done up.

If you have a button with four holes in it, traditionally you cross the threads

Sewing on the front buttons.

diagonally across the button although two parallel sets of stitches will function just as well.

When you have finished going through the button, bring the thread up to just below the button and then wrap the thread firmly round the shank from the button down to the jacket front.

Take the needle through to the back of the jacket and fasten off the thread with a couple of small back stitches.

Before you start stitching the buttons on the cuffs, make sure that the vent is sitting straight. As these buttons don't fasten up, there is no need to leave the stitches loose to make a shank.

Taking the thread along to the next cuff button.

Sewing on the cuff buttons.

Once you have sewn the first cuff button on, do not cut the thread; simply take your needle through to the inside of the cuff and slide the needle between fabric and lining to the next button position.

Continue in this manner until all the buttons have been stitched on.

Look carefully at the whole garment and check for chalk marks. Using a soft clothes brush, brush any remaining chalk away gently before doing any further pressing.

Final Press

Remove the basting holding the pleat in the lining in place. Press the lining along the pleat line to remove any indents the basting may have caused.

Remove the stitches holding the buttonholes in place and press any indents from around the buttonhole.

If necessary, steam any crumples which may have occurred whilst you have been buttoning the jacket.

And there you have it, a finished jacket made in the traditional tailored way. This jacket will last for many years and whenever you wear it you will feel proud of what you have accomplished.

I hope you have enjoyed making the jacket as much as I have enjoyed showing you how to do it.

Appendix

Lapel Shaper Pattern

See Chapter 7. Use a large piece of card
and draw out a full-size grid where each
square measures 2.5cm (1in). Transfer
the pattern and then cut the shape out.
You will be able to mark up your lapels
without any problems every time you
make a jacket.

If you punch a hole in your pattern
you can hang it up so that it does not
get damaged.

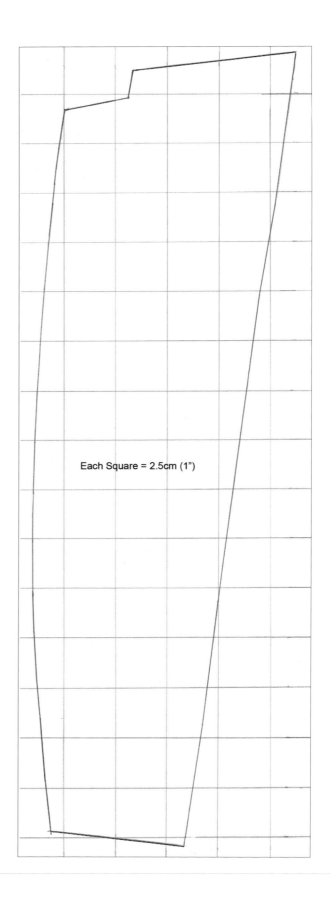

Each Square = 2.5cm (1")

Glossary of Tailoring Terms

Balance marks - Positions marked on either side of a seam to position two pieces together, this could be as notches at the side of the pieces or tailor tacks.

Banger - See Point presser and clapper.

Basting - The tailor's word for tacking.

Basting out - The process of laying together all the layers of the jacket for the start of the construction of the jacket up to and including the front facing.

Basting under - The second stage of the process for getting the jacket in one piece after the machining stage of the front facing.

Bias - The bias or grosgrain of the fabric is at a 45° angle to the straight grain of the cloth. Fabric cut at this angle will have a stretch to it and makes perfect bias binding or piping cord covering.

Break point - The point of the front of the jacket where the centre front turns back to form the lapel.

Break line - The edge of the lapel that is formed when the fabric turns back.

Bridle - A piece of fabric, usually lining which is placed on to the inside of the break line on the straight grain, to prevent the break line stretching out.

Bum lay - The cut edge of the cloth which is not level when laid out ready for cutting out.

Cabbage - The name given to any spare or leftover fabric.

Coat - In the tailoring workrooms a jacket is referred to as a coat. The coat we are used to is known as an overcoat.

Collar Stand - The piece of the collar which stands up around the back of the neck.

Collar Fall - The piece of the collar which lays flat or falls over the shoulder.

Cross grain - *See* Bias.

Crown of the sleeve - The top or head of the sleeve where most of the fullness is.

Drawing the collar - The process of stitching the top collar to the front facing around the neckline.

Forearm seam - The short seam on the front of the sleeve.

Gimp - Thick thread used to pad out a buttonhole.

Hind arm seam - The long seam at the back of a sleeve.

Inlays - A variable seam allowance used in the tailoring workrooms to allow for alterations on the jacket.

Jets - The lips of the pocket. On a jetted pocket.

Mungo - *See* Cabbage.

Mungo Man - The person who comes to take away and recycle leftover cuttings of cloth.

Nap - The finish on certain cloth which means it has to be cut in one direction only. Velvet is a good example of this.

Notches - *See* Balance marks.

Plastron - The reinforced area of the chest. This piece fills the gap between the shoulder and the bustline. The name is taken from a suit of armour.

Point presser and clapper - A wooden tool used to absorb steam when pressing. Setting the cloth immediately. It is also used for pressing into corners.

Quarter off - The name given to the position of stitching which is located 6mm (¼") in from the edge of the jacket or pockets.

Roll of the cloth - The excess amount of fabric allowed to prevent the front edge, collar etcetera from pulling tight or dog earring.

Silesia - The trade name for a strong cotton fabric used in pockets.

Tailor tack - Sometimes known as mark stitches or stitch marks. These stitches mark positions on the garment which cannot be marked by notches or snips.

Tailor's weight - A long flat piece of metal used to hold down the pattern whilst the edge of the pattern is drawn on to the cloth with chalk.

Toile - A mock-up garment usually made in calico for fitting. The word toile is from the French word for working.

Truing the pattern - The last stage of doing an alteration, where you make the pattern as near to the original shape whilst including your alteration.

T-zone - The shape of the main canvasses going through the front of the jacket. When the two side are placed together it looks just like a capital T.

Index

basting out 82–91
  applying the facing 87–91
  bridle 85, 98
  canvassing the jacket 82–84
  fastening the pocket bag 87
  marking the lapels for pad stitching 84–86
  marking the jacket front 87–89
  securing the jacket edges 89–90
basting under 91–94
  basting the edges 91–92
  lining in 92–94
buttonholes 115–118
  buttonhole stitch 117
  making the bar tack 117
  marking the buttonhole 116
  positioning the gimp 117
  preparing the hole 116
  preparing the thread 116
  shaping the buttonhole 117–118
buttoning the jacket 121–122

canvasses
  cutting out 78–81
  joining up 81–82
  pad stitching 81
collar 96–100
  drawing the collar 100
  top collar 99–100
  undercollar 96–98
choosing the pattern 20–21
cutting out
  canvasses 78–79
  main fabric 49–53
lining 55–58
  toile 22–23

equipment 8–12

fitting the toile 26–28
  the collar 28
  excess fabric in seams 27
  excess fabric not in seams 27
  fabric pulling tight 28
  levels 27
  marking the pocket position 28

hand finishing 112–118
  collar 100
  lining 114–115
  making up the armhole 112–113
hand stitches 13–18
  basting 14
  felling 15–16
  herringbone 18
  pad stitching 15–18
  prick stitching 15
  slip stitch 14
  tailor tacks 53–54
  thread tracing 15

joining the pieces
  for the toile 23–26
  for the jacket 60–61
  for the lining 63

introduction 6

lining in 92–94

materials 12–13

pad stitching 15–17, 81, 86, 97
pattern 20–21
  centre front panel 55–56
pattern alterations 30–46
  bust increase for larger cup sizes 33–35
  lengthening or shortening jacket sleeves 37–38

  shoulder seam in the wrong place 35–37
  sway back 40–42
  taking in seams 38–40
  truing the pattern 42–46
  waistline/bustline in the wrong place 30–32
pinning
  pattern to main fabric 52–53
  seams 60–61
piping front facing 63–64
plastron
  setting the plastron 94
pockets 66–76
  flapped pocket 70–72
  jetted pocket 67–70
  preparation for pockets 66–67
  tailors patch pocket 74–76
  welt pocket 72–74
pressing
  final press 122
  pressing off 120–121
  seams 61–62

shoulders
  marking up 94
  shoulder pads 112–113
  shoulder seams 94
sleeve 102–110
  lining in the sleeve 105–106
  making up the vent 102–104
  sleeve placement 106–109
  sleeve seam 105
  sleeve wrap 109–110

toile 21–28
  cutting and marking 22–23
  fitting the toile 26–28
  making up 23–26
t-zone
  cutting out 78–79

RELATED TITLES FROM CROWOOD

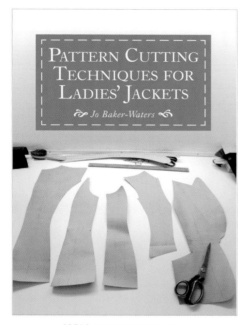

ISBN: 978 1 78500 177 2

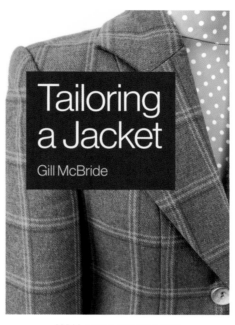

ISBN: 978 1 78500 7 835

ISBN: 978 1 78500 447 6

ISBN: 978 1 84797 373 3